DATE DUE

JUN – – 2006	Arrival Date		

DEMCO 38-296

Managing a Crisis

MANAGING

A CRISIS

A Practical Guide

Tom Curtin

with

Daniel Hayman and Naomi Husein

First published 2005 by
PALGRAVE MACMILLAN
Houndmills, Basingstoke, Hampshire RG21 6XS and
175 Fifth Avenue, New York, N.Y. 10010
Companies and representatives throughout the world

PALGRAVE MACMILLAN is the global academic imprint of the Palgrave Macmillan division of St. Martin's Press, LLC and of Palgrave Macmillan Ltd. Macmillan® is a registered trademark in the United States, United Kingdom and other countries. Palgrave is a registered trademark in the European Union and other countries.

ISBN 1–4039–4322–2

This book is printed on paper suitable for recycling and made from fully managed and sustained forest sources.

A catalogue record for this book is available from the British Library.

A catalog record for this book is available from the Library of Congress.

10 9 8 7 6 5 4 3 2 1
14 13 12 11 10 09 08 07 06 05

Printed and bound in Great Britain by
Creative Print & Design (Wales), Ebbw Vale

For Fiona, Peter, Susan, Margaret and Mahmud

CONTENTS

INTRODUCTION

Most organisations place great store on their reputation. They see that companies with a good reputation have strong brands and this can mean greater profitability. In addition, it helps with credibility and credit rating. It also makes recruitment less difficult if the company's reputation is solid and good; those with good reputations tend to attract good people.

A badly handled crisis can damage or ruin that reputation. It hits internal morale and can impinge on productivity among employees. It is also deeply uncomfortable for management; no one wants to play golf with the CEO whose company is a major polluter.

So, there are real commercial reasons for managing crises well. A brand which is supported by many millions of dollars of advertising can be damaged overnight. It is an investment in a word, a name, an image. Its insurance policy is good crisis management strategies.

Managing a crisis well can actually bring benefits. In the case of the Kegworth disaster for British Midland, sales for the company rose after the crisis because it had been open, honest and sympathetic to those who had been injured and the bereaved.

Johnson & Johnson found that its branded analgesic Tylenol actually gained in sales after it had been open and honest when faced with a blackmailer who threatened to poison the products.

But when Perrier decided that the tiny trace levels of benzene in its bottled mineral water were of no real consequence, it was proved wrong and the private company was taken over by Nestlé. Shell, Monsanto and the nuclear industry will all testify to how a badly managed crisis can damage not just the brand but the fabric of the company.

In essence, manage a crisis well and your brand is enhanced; manage it badly and you can lose the company.

The rules of the game are very simple:

1. Look carefully at the signals. What is the worst-case scenario? – that is probably what you are heading for.

2. A little expense now saves a fortune later on.
3. Don't rush – the person who made time made plenty of it. A deadline is the great enemy of good planning in delicate issues.
4. Overcompensate – to be accused is to be guilty. This is grossly unfair, but then so is life.
5. Things will get worse before they get better, so the ostrich syndrome – hoping it will go away if you ignore it – is not an option. It is here to stay.

Yet how often, as this book will illustrate, do we see these simple rules flouted?

Handle a crisis well and your reputation, sales and profits will all be enhanced. Handle it badly and you risk losing the company. This book attempts to give some guidelines on how to achieve the former.

Acknowledgements

We would like to thank a number of people who have helped with the book, giving us their time, support and advice. Thanks to Kevin Howlett for his work on the case studies within the book, Sue Poole for her help and fantastic organisational skills and all the staff at Green Issues Communications who have given their support. Our thanks especially to Stephen Rutt of the publishers and to those at IMD, especially Jacques Horovitz, Roger Hooijberg, Victoria Giorginni and Sonia Dutoit. Of course, our final thanks go to our friends and families who were there for us throughout.

The authors and publisher would like to thank Mirrorpix for permission to use copyright material from the *Daily Mirror* on page 44.
Every effort has been made to trace all the copyright holders but if any have been inadvertently overlooked the publishers will be pleased to make the necessary arrangements at the first opportunity.

SECTION A

What Makes a Crisis

CHAPTER 1

The Three Types of Crisis

In essence, there are three types of crisis. First, there are those such as plane crashes, accidents, spillages of chemicals, product defects and so on, which *befall* a company.

Second, there are those that are *manufactured*. For example, the *Brent Spar* would have caused no controversy for Shell had Greenpeace not become involved.

Finally, there are those crises which *escalate from an accident*. For example, when the Chernobyl nuclear power plant exploded, the green groups were quick to seize on it as a means of attacking the nuclear industry throughout the world.

Accidents will happen

Crises that arise from major accidents are often the most tragic but the easiest to deal with.

THE SWISSAIR CRASH

In 1998, flight SR111 took off from New York. After one hour, the plane had disappeared and 229 people had died. The cause of the crash remains a mystery, but numerous conspiracy theories have been put forward.

On the night, Swissair reacted with commendable haste and immediately made information available. It held regular press briefings and made sure that it passed on information in a humane and systematic manner. It was open and frank with the media, but, more importantly, made $20,000 available to each victim's family almost immediately, so they could visit the scene.

This generous gesture received a warm response. The company was also open on its website and hosted daily press conferences for the media. For grieving parents, friends and family, this became a constant and reliable source of information. Swissair did not try to blame or fight what had happened, but simply accepted the situation and thought of the victims.

Analysis

This is almost a classic model for how to handle a crisis well. Swissair was very well prepared. It reacted swiftly and sympathetically to those who had been bereaved; it handled the media well, with updates on its website and regular press conferences. The crisis was handled and blew over and, importantly, the brand was left unscathed.

Ironically, these types of crisis – which involve a large loss of life – are the easiest to prepare for. Everyone knows that an aeroplane risks crashing and, therefore, it is easy – although not always – to have the necessary procedures in place.

Also falling into this category are those incidents where there is a problem with a product. Here, as we will find later with Tylenol, Nike and other products, the company has no choice but to react quickly. Sunny Delight did not.

SUNNY DELIGHT

The year 1998 saw the release of an exciting new brand on the market. Sunny Delight offered kids all the excitement of the popular soft drink brands but, supposedly, with none of the negative health impacts. Mums were sold on this bright sparkling drink – surely orange juice could not be this sexy.

Within months of its launch, Sunny Delight had become the biggest selling soft drink in the UK, after Coke and Pepsi. Sales stood at £160 million a year. It was truly a marketing phenomenon, as supermarkets ran out of stock and children couldn't get enough of this new beverage.

Soon, however, the appeal wore off as the much-trumpeted, healthy qualities of the drink came under fire. The brand was knocked as national newspapers and consumer groups woke up to the high sugar content of the supposedly healthy drink. Confidence in the drink was all but shattered when it was revealed that a five-year-old girl had turned orange after drinking excessive amounts, almost 1.5 litres a day. This coincided with an embarrassing Christmas TV advert depicting a snowman drinking the ubiquitous brew and promptly turning orange.

The brand was attacked from all sides, from the health watchdog and the food commission to BBC's *Watchdog* programme and Radio 4. Sales slumped, the revenue ran dry and eventually Procter & Gamble were forced to sell the brand.

Analysis

So what went wrong? Two things: the first mistake was to oversell the product, or 'over-claim' the healthy qualities of the drink. Procter & Gamble had seriously misjudged the sophisticated consumer who was now more wary of corporate power and less willing to trust implicitly. In 2004, Coca-Cola ran into the same problem with Desani – which was filtered tap water in a fancy bottle – sold at the same price as bottled water, usually derived from natural sources.

Having been deemed to have misled the public, the management behind Sunny Delight then made its second mistake; to hide and stay quiet. The team behind the project had developed a reputation for being secretive and unresponsive to public concerns. This is something which Jon Walsh, Sunny Delight brand manager, admitted: 'We didn't enter the debate. We stayed in our little castle thinking if we don't say anything, the debate will go away.' It was as if the creators believed that the public would simply forget the negative images and once again be attracted back to the product. By the company not explaining itself, the public were left to believe the worst about Sunny Delight.

Consumers will no longer take what companies say for granted – they will test it, quiz it and then make their own judgements. Certainly marketing and advertising helps, but it cannot overcome a product problem, especially when the product or brand behind it hits a crisis. We live in a world which is less deferential to the god of marketing and much more self-aware.

Compare Sunny Delight's behaviour with the actions of a much smaller company which had a similar problem.

ODWALLA

Odwalla's fruit juice drinks were extremely popular in the 1980s and the early 1990s. The company had grown at a rapid rate year on year and had achieved a high level of customer loyalty and attachment to its brand.

However, the company was thrown into crisis when US officials discovered a link between Odwalla's apple juice drink and the *E. coli* bacterium. Over 60 people were taken ill after consuming the drink and, more tragically, a child died. Immediately the company's shares fell sharply, by over a third, customers sued and sales stood at 10 per cent of their pre-crisis figure.

Odwalla sprung into action and accepted responsibility. Even before the cases were confirmed, the CEO, Stephen Williamson, recalled the product from the shops. He was also interviewed by a number of different media and always took the opportunity to express sadness for the victims and their families. The company wanted to appear responsive and responsible. As a gesture, Odwalla also agreed to pay medical costs. By answering the concerns of customers, the company had begun to win back their support.

However, the company did not stop there, it made sure that customers and employees were kept up to date with the news via a number of communications tools, including a website which was established almost immediately. In addition it quickly changed its processes to adopt the safest and cleanest method for making the juice – again a responsive move, taking to heart the questions asked of the company.

Analysis

The company managed to keep much of the trust and brand identification it had established with its customer base. By putting its customers first in these difficult circumstances, rather than watching the bottom line, the company was seen to be actually taking care of its customers – which one would admit is rare today. Those values which had established Odwalla were able to bring it through the crisis and recover sales.

Odwalla learned the first rule of crisis management:

If you think you have a problem, then you probably have one.

React accordingly.

If someone else thinks you have a problem, then you definitely have.

React unilaterally.

Manufacturing a crisis

The green groups and non-governmental organisations (NGOs) are, for the most part, unelected and therefore unaccountable. The huge noise – and the ensuing crises – against projects such as *Brent Spar* and genetically modified organisms (GMOs) are orchestrated and managed by just a few people. Certainly they are successful in changing public opinion on these issues, but this is not a fault of the system. This is the fault of the companies and they cannot shirk this. Certainly, the media will play its part, but that is known and expected. Politicians will play their part, but their behaviour, again, is both known and predictable.

The case of Monsanto and Greenpeace shows how a project which was scientifically valid was knocked totally off course by a crisis generated by Greenpeace. Although Monsanto did all the running and had huge and powerful political backing (the president of the US and the UK's prime minister), it still lost the war, thanks to the crisis tactics employed by green activists, shining a harsh and alarmist spotlight on the issue.

MONSANTO AND GREENPEACE

Greenpeace is vehemently opposed to the use of GMOs. In fact, so strong is its opposition that it does not believe that any research should be undertaken in this area. Although the research has the backing of governments, Greenpeace is not interested in the results: it has made up its mind that it wants no truck with GMOs. Full stop.

And it uses powerful emotional arguments, that is,' Frankenstein Food'. Monsanto, on the other hand, tried to appeal to rational arguments (incidentally, the similarities between its approach and that of Shell, in the *Brent Spar* case explained later, are remarkable).

Monsanto ran a huge public relations and advertising campaign in an attempt to lay the facts in front of the people and allow them to make a rational decision. In the industry magazine, *PR Week*, Monsanto's PR agency Good Relations said it wanted to move the debate 'onto a rational footing'. The debate was lost at this point. Putting food for your children into a shopping basket is not a rational decision. It is an emotional decision and one where the vast majority of people – no matter how well educated on the facts and the rationality of the arguments – are not willing to take risks. To quote the old maxim of the experienced newspaper editor: 'When in doubt, leave it out'.

Those speaking against Monsanto were a wide-ranging group. On a BBC *Newsnight* programme, Monsanto put forward its spokespersons, but Greenpeace was not to be seen. Instead there were academics (independent, without doubt) and the chief executive of the frozen food retailer Iceland (the irony of a spokesperson for one form of food modification – freezing – speaking out against another form of modification was lost on the audience and obviously on the BBC). The result was a total victory for Greenpeace who were not even there.

Analysis

So keen was Monsanto to show how fair it was being in the debate on GM foods that it actually printed Greenpeace's web address on the advertisements. By doing this, what was Monsanto saying to the world? Here are some thoughts:

- By far the most important stakeholder we have is Greenpeace, more important than our employees, our scientists, our customers, the politicians and regulators.
- In particular they are more important than the independent scientists who undertook much of the research work for us on GM foods; ignore these people and listen instead to Greenpeace.
- The minute we convince Greenpeace that GM food is safe, and this won't be long, they will endorse our stand.

Even if these thoughts were not in the minds of the Monsanto communications experts – and no doubt they were not, even if they should have been – this is the strong perception which came across. Greenpeace was, of course, delighted and redoubled its efforts to stop even testing.

This is a typical manufactured crisis. An unelected NGO seizes on a cause and escalates it into a crisis. No one has died, yet the furore caused by GM foods is much greater than that caused by the Swissair crash, with its loss of more than 100 lives, and appeals to the media and the public in an alarmist and photogenic way. The use of boiler suits and gas masks when activists destroyed crops was a clever 'branding' tactic – using the PR world's rules against itself.

However, the damage to brand and reputation is huge. In the UK, GM foods have almost become an 'anti-brand', with the trucks of one of the country's largest retailers, Marks & Spencer, proudly displaying signs that the company does not use GM foods, and many more supermarkets and brands have followed suit.

Crises from accidents

With the Swissair crash, the company performed well and survived and, indeed for some time afterwards, thrived. (It took the attack on the Twin Towers in New York – which led to a sudden drop in passenger numbers – to force Swissair into administration.)

So, if one is open and transparent, one can recover from a crisis. But what happens if one isn't?

CHERNOBYL – DEATH OF THE NUCLEAR INDUSTRY?

Chernobyl was the site of a nuclear power station in the Ukraine. It was built to a design that the west had deemed unsafe because if it were not managed properly, there was a risk – in extreme circumstances – that the reactor could explode.

The accident at the Chernobyl nuclear power station took place on the night of April 25/26 1986. The plan was to test whether the turbines could produce sufficient energy to keep the coolant pumps running in the event of a loss of power until the emergency generator was activated.

In order to conduct this test, the safety systems were deliberately switched off. For the test, the reactor had to be powered down to 25 per cent of its capacity. For reasons which are still not known, the reactor power level fell to less than 1 per cent. The power therefore had to be slowly increased. But 30 seconds after the start of the test, there was a sudden and unexpected power surge. The reactor's safety systems, which should have stopped the chain reaction, failed.

Almost instantly, the power level and temperature rose many times over and there was a violent explosion. The 1000-tonne sealing cap on the reactor building was blown off and at 2000°C the fuel rods melted. The fire that followed meant that radioactive particles were sent into the atmosphere. The graphite covering of the reactor then ignited. In the ensuing inferno, the radioactive fission products released during the core meltdown were sucked up into the atmosphere.

The accident killed 30 people, including 28 from radiation exposure. A further 209 on site were treated for acute radiation poisoning and, among these, 134 cases were confirmed (all of whom recovered).

However, the plume of radioactive particles moved through the atmosphere and was soon picked up in routine monitoring in Scandinavia. It took some days to figure out what had happened and eventually the Ukrainian authorities had to admit they had suffered an accident.

Analysis

The consequences were immense. The radiation travelled extensively and was soon deposited all over western Europe. For many years, sheep farmers in Wales were not allowed to graze their sheep on some areas which had been contaminated.

Although the economic, medical and sociological effects on the Ukraine were devastating, the whole of the nuclear industry was tarnished by the brush of Chernobyl. Although western Europe rightly said that a similar accident could not happen in the west, the green groups scorned this. They pointed to the secrecy surrounding the explosion as being indicative of the industry's secrecy worldwide; they pointed to the catastrophic effect and asked: Can you guarantee that something similar will never happen in the west? No one can guarantee that, especially with the shadow of Three Mile Island at the back of everyone's mind.

Since Chernobyl, almost no nuclear power stations have been constructed in the west. And this is a huge potential crisis in the making for the energy-hungry western economies. From the accident, a real crisis has been manufactured.

Of the three types of crisis, it is apparent that those which are manufactured can bring the most lasting damage. They are also the most difficult to predict and plan for.

CHAPTER 2

Evolution of a Crisis: the Crisis Curve

Most large companies, as part of their risk assessment, undertake an assessment of how likely it is that a particular crisis will hit them. It is an extremely valuable exercise and should be undertaken with due rigour. This exercise is outlined in Chapter 3. However, anyone who takes comfort that they now fully understand the total implications of a crisis is naive indeed. Certainly, one can look to many indicators, for example the vulnerability of the industry to environmental damage. However, these indicators are not, in themselves, totally reliable and some highly crisis-prone industries continue without a crisis for decades. When the management of crises goes badly wrong, it is usually because the corporation has either ignored or failed to recognise the significance of some of the indicators.

A crisis is like an earthquake – it is difficult to predict when and if it will strike. However, seismologists today look to certain indicators in an effort to predict earthquakes. Volcanologists too now have good indicators based on geological phenomena of when a volcano is likely to erupt. However, none of these are precise sciences.

It is therefore important to understand how a crisis evolves and the 'crisis curve' is a good means of illustrating this evolution.

The crisis curve

The crisis curve plots the time elapsing against the intensity of the crisis – effectively mapping its lifeline. To illustrate this, we will use the case of the *Brent Spar*.

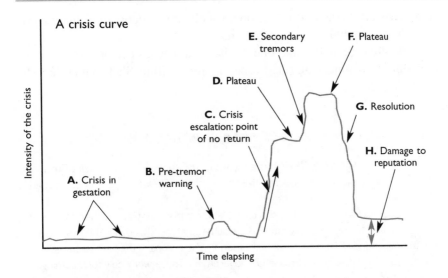

A crisis curve

Intensity of the crisis

Time elapsing

A. Crisis in gestation

B. Pre-tremor warning

C. Crisis escalation: point of no return

D. Plateau

E. Secondary tremors

F. Plateau

G. Resolution

H. Damage to reputation

Point A: Crisis in gestation

Consider the following. In the North Sea to the north of Germany and the east of Britain, there is a redundant oil installation. It is not near any people and, for sound environmental reasons, the company which manages it wishes to dispose of it. It has taken all the soundings with technical experts on safety on an environmental impact and all are agreed that the best way to get rid of this installation is to dispose of it deep at sea in the North Atlantic. After years of detailed and technical studies, the government scientists are also content that this is the best way forward. As well as all the rational arguments, there is also an emotional argument. During the last two world wars, numerous tons of shipping went to the bottom of the sea with no apparent environmental impact. One more oil installation – almost totally clean of any polluting materials – surely could not make much difference.

You have been asked by Shell to advise on the implications of this.

The honest answer is that most communication professionals would say that there should be very few. After all, the installation is not near anyone – no one lives there. It is also far away from the main media centres of Europe. The likelihood of an event becoming a major news story is in inverse proportion to its proximity to the capital city. (Stories from Washington DC have a lot more currency than those from Seattle.)

And it has all the technical tick boxes including support from the government. There should not be a problem.

Yet, *Brent Spar* became one of the great causes célèbres of the environmental movement and had repercussions within Shell which are still felt to this day.

BRENT SPAR – *POINT A*

Brent Spar started life in the 1970s as a means of transporting oil to tankers. But, by the 1980s, new technology had rendered the *Spar* obsolete. Shell, the *Spar's* operator, had to dispose of it.

After some four years of technical, safety, environment and other studies, the company came to the conclusion that disposal deep at sea was by far the best option. It was the safest and most environmentally friendly. The company then set about getting all the necessary permissions from the UK government. These were duly forthcoming.

At this stage, we are at point A of the crisis curve. Certainly, Shell was aware that environmental issues were rising in the public consciousness, but it had chosen the best practical environmental option. As Eric Faulds, head of construction at Shell UK stated: 'We look at problems and come up with balanced solutions, based on science and facts alone. We can't base it on emotions.'

By the 1980s, Greenpeace was an organisation in crisis. It had become not a lean, mean campaigning organisation, but a fairly substantive corporate bureaucracy. It had moved on from the days of dinghies harassing nuclear-powered submarines and was now a more sedate organisation. However, as noted later, there is fierce corporate competition for members (sales) between NGOs and Greenpeace was losing out. It needed something high profile and sensational in order to improve its brand.

Greenpeace's siege of the *Brent Spar* was dreamt up ahead of a meeting of European politicians to discuss the North Sea. The symbolic value was there for all to see. This was Greenpeace attempting to go back to its old-fashioned, high-profile stunts. It was looking for dramatic images to recapture some of the support it had lost over the years, following a run of unsuccessful and low-profile campaigns.

Plans were drawn up by German activists in April 1995. The board of Greenpeace approved the plans the next day. Greenpeace then began planning for the operation. This involved bringing in climbers and necessary equipment for the campaign. This stage took just two weeks.

On April 27 the Greenpeace boat set sail carrying volunteers determined to climb onto the rig. On April 30 Greenpeace boarded the *Brent Spar*. Essentially Greenpeace had caught Shell by surprise. When Shell had become aware that they had set sail, it called an urgent meeting to discuss what could possibly happen as a result. Shell's security adviser at the time said 'the worst-case scenarios were discussed, but before any plans could be implemented they [Greenpeace] boarded'. Shell was not prepared in any way for what was about to happen.

Point B: Pre-tremor warning

We are now at point B on the crisis curve. The *Spar* is occupied by activists. What should Shell do now?

Of course, all this is easy in hindsight, but this blip on the curve cannot and should not be ignored. There were two options open to Shell:

1. attempt to remove the trespassers
2. ignore them until they went away.

Shell chose the former option. This was a key decision – from this point on there is no turning back.

Suppose Shell had decided to leave the protesters on the *Spar*, what would have happened? The main news angle had been documented, boarding the *Spar* was already well covered and the media is a fickle beast – it bores very easily. After a month on the *Spar* and possibly sooner, the media would have got thoroughly bored. After all, news is just news once: the headline 'Greenpeace protesters still on *Brent Spar*' is not exactly riveting news.

Point C: Escalation: point of no return

Most organisations do not walk away from problems, they solve them. There was a project and there was a project plan, so Shell decided to take Greenpeace on.

Greenpeace is probably one of the best public relations agencies in the world and when it boarded the *Spar*, it brought £300,000 worth of broadcast equipment on board. Within a few hours of boarding, it began broadcasting live from the rig. Reports were beamed into the homes of millions as Greenpeace, in effect, launched its own live newsroom. Greenpeace had also set up a press office onshore, to make sure that its message was heard first and heard most. Greenpeace was able to dictate the news agenda. It was Greenpeace who supplied the 'facts' and therefore determined the spin on the story.

By the third week, Shell was making its way through legal documents searching for a plan which would allow it legally to evict the 'squatters' from the *Brent Spar*. On May 23, just over three weeks after Greenpeace had boarded, Shell moved to get the Greenpeace activists off the rig. Naturally Greenpeace alerted the world's media, who were now in the North Sea in huge numbers. Shell commandeered one of the largest oil rigs in the area to launch its attack on the *Spar*. A pitched battle ensued, with Shell's security force being repelled back by Greenpeace activists. Because the security staff were in a

suspended cradle as they tried to board the *Spar*, this made highly entertaining television. It was classic entertainment – and the media has a huge entertainment agenda – in
the best Hollywood style. Greenpeace retaliated by throwing smoke bombs at the
advancing 'troops'. Shell eventually reclaimed the *Spar* and the world's media recorded
the activists being taken off *Brent Spar*.

Point D: Plateau

At this stage, the battle of perception was totally lost. Greenpeace became
the David, Shell the Goliath. With images of 'have-a-go heroes/plucky
campaigners', call them what you will, in the clutches of an all-powerful
opponent, it was not difficult to predict on which side the sympathies of
the public would fall. Shell's carefully nurtured reputation was in tatters.

Greenpeace certainly had achieved its first aim – to raise the whole issue
of sea dumping in the minds of the public. But Shell felt that it too had won
a victory for itself and the rule of law. After all, Greenpeace's trespassing
was illegal. The company now settled down to get on with its project. But
the battle was not over yet, as Greenpeace opened a second front.

The German media in particular had covered the *Brent Spar* story with great zeal. They
had strongly taken the Greenpeace line. Germany has one of the largest green parties in
Europe and it regularly polls up to 20 per cent of the vote. Greenpeace drew on this
sympathy and began to organise boycotts of Shell products.

It also kept up the pressure around the *Brent Spar* by providing ongoing media
opportunities for the cameras. Shell was an unwitting and willing accomplice to these
antics. For example, if a small Greenpeace boat neared the *Brent Spar*, Shell defended
its property by firing high-powered water cannons. Greenpeace made a number of
daring forays into these dangerous waters, narrowly escaping being hit by the full force
of these cannons.

This made for great television. Media boats were all around, capturing every
moment, every shot fired and every narrow escape by Greenpeace. If the media
went away or were not available, Greenpeace used its own broadcast equipment to
record the events and then sent the video tapes by helicopter to the studios of the
world's press.

Greenpeace knew that it was winning the propaganda war. However, it did not rest
on its laurels. The campaign group organised a number of carefully stage-managed events
designed to be easily and powerfully broadcastable. The most memorable of these
pictured the media going out on the Greenpeace tug to ride through the spray generated from the water cannons. Importantly, it placed the media in the same position in
relation to Shell as Greenpeace. Suddenly, viewers were seeing events directly through
the eyes of Greenpeace activists. They had been transferred into their world – they
were in effect joining the Greenpeace campaign.

At this stage, Greenpeace began to look for friends and allies and found a most unusual one in the shape of the German Lutheran Church, which has a boycotting committee, which gave its support to the campaign to boycott Shell products.

Despite the boycotts and the antics at sea, Shell must have seen a calmer scene. The *Spar* was being prepared for disposal and had been rigged with explosives. Certainly there was noise, but the company held a firm nerve. It was used to controversy and, without doubt, once the *Spar* was disposed of, the fuss would blow over and that would be the end of the matter. It could then go about the business of repairing its reputation and brand.

Point E: Secondary tremors

For Greenpeace, there was a real fear that Shell might be right. It needed to up the stakes fairly urgently before the story went cold. And the all-important meeting of EC ministers was fast looming. It was vital for Greenpeace that its campaign climaxed at this time.

June 8 saw the arrival of politicians for the North Sea conference. At the same time, boycotts of Shell merchandise were taking effect and protesters had camped outside the conference centre. By the second week of June, Shell's takings in Germany were down by 30 per cent. The political heat was turning up.

On June 16, Greenpeace ratcheted up the pressure even more by attempting its most daring stunt. The pressure group flew a helicopter out to the *Brent Spar* and dropped activists down onto the oil rig. The scenes were dramatic as the helicopter perilously ducked and dived, manoeuvring its way through the spray of the water cannons. This was real danger and there was no doubt who the public would be supporting. Activists eventually managed to land on the *Spar*, setting up base once more in their temporary home. Activists remained on board while Shell continuously fired its water guns at the *Brent Spar*. Shell had become embroiled in a siege. The company was trying everything to smoke out the squatters. And it was all captured by the cameras.

But the campaign had now reached a bigger political stage. In the media and in parliament, John Major, the British prime minister, consistently and vociferously backed Shell's plans for deep sea disposal. He was attacked by the German Chancellor Helmut Kohl, who publicly berated him for his defence of Shell UK. German public opinion had moved so far against Shell that it had become virtually impossible for the chancellor not to express some level of opposition to the company's actions.

Over the following two nights there were incidents of terrorist activity against Shell targets in Germany. Two garages were hit by so-called ecoterrorists. Shell was now seriously rattled.

On June 20, Shell sent security staff on board the *Brent Spar* forcibly to evict the Greenpeace campaigners. They succeeded. However, this represented something of a Pyrrhic victory.

The *Spar* was ready for disposal – its anchors were lifted and it was ready to make the journey to the North Atlantic. Shell – and Greenpeace – could begin to see the beginning of the end.

Following the bombings in Germany, Chris Fay, Chairman of Shell UK, was confronted by his colleagues from other countries. He was essentially told to abandon the *Brent Spar* operation. Public opinion, particularly in northern European countries, had forced Shell's executive to consider this option seriously, regardless of the implications.

On June 20, Chris Fay went back to London and called the Department of Trade and Industry to inform them of what he was about to do. The crisis then took one final twist. Clearly the message of Shell's decision had not reached Number 10 Downing Street. As John Major, the prime minister, stepped up to the dispatch box at Prime Minister's Questions (a then twice weekly chance for MPs to grill the prime minister on issues of the day), he defended Shell UK's decision to dump the *Brent Spar* in the Atlantic. Shell's real decision was later made public, undermining John Major's position.

Chris Fay, chairman of Shell UK: 'We did things too properly, we covered all the scientific, technical and legalistic angles. However, we didn't take into account hearts and emotions.'

Points G and H: Plateau and resolution

Following Shell's decision, the media soon lost interest and the curve heads towards low intensity. Fifteen years later few people know the details of the *Brent Spar*. If we were to look at the crisis curve for *Brent Spar*, it would probably look something like this.

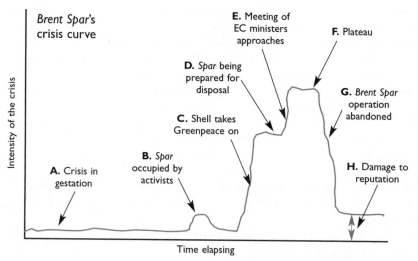

Brent Spar's crisis curve

E. Meeting of EC ministers approaches

F. Plateau

D. *Spar* being prepared for disposal

G. *Brent Spar* operation abandoned

C. Shell takes Greenpeace on

B. *Spar* occupied by activists

A. Crisis in gestation

H. Damage to reputation

Intensity of the crisis

Time elapsing

Analysis

Shell – one of the oligarchs of the oil industry, indeed of world industry – had been badly damaged. The damage to its reputation is measured as Point H of the graph. This means that the organisation is now more vulnerable to future crises. And so, when accusations of corruption in Nigeria were made against the company, its enemies piled in again. This time Greenpeace found a new ally in the shape of The Body Shop chain, an international company with a high-profile, green consciousness. The next crisis followed the same curve as the first one and again more reputation damage was done.

Shell has worked hard since then to repair its reputation, and there has been reorganisation of its board structure. But a further crisis hit in 2004 when it was revealed that oil resources were understated, leading to the resignation of the chairman.

The lesson from the crisis curve is simple: if you do not handle a crisis well, you will stay in crisis mode for a long time.

CHAPTER 3

Predicting a Crisis

The sheer size of today's corporations – and they are getting bigger – means that they are more vulnerable than ever to crises, either from natural origins or those manufactured. As noted earlier, crises are extremely difficult to predict. This problem is exacerbated by the trend in the 1970s and 80s to develop managers as specialists. The finance director knows about finance and little else; similarly the marketing director, the technology director and the operations director all have their specialist fields. This smokestack approach – like tennis balls in a box – leads to gaps in the management structure. This means that a finance director, driven rightly by profits and earnings per share, would often lose sight of the bigger picture. However, in the 1990s, this trend began to be reversed and the manager as a generalist as well as a specialist began to come into vogue. MBA programmes widen their focus and smaller programmes, such as the excellent Programme for Executive Development as run by the IMD in Lausanne, produce managers who are far more rounded than they were previously.

This rounding of management knowledge is an ideal net in which to capture emerging crises. Ideally, senior or general managers should have a working knowledge of politics, the media, reputation and brand values, and social and corporate social responsibility (CSR). Unfortunately, these are rather vague topics and whilst courses such as MBAs and others can do much to address this, they are not formal enough to put in place a proper management procedure. Whilst it is not in the remit of this book to cover corporate social responsibility, it is within this area that the nascent crises can be identified and nipped in the bud before they become real problems.

Checklist

1 Are all managers aware of the power and influence of:
   - Politics and the political environment in which they operate
   - The media and its realms and influence and how to deal with it
   - The value of a company's reputation
   - Stakeholder management
   - Corporate social responsibility?
2 Is there a formal mechanism – such as a questionnaire – by which managers can identify those areas they think might be problems for the company?
3 Is there a procedure for analysing and auditing this information and acting where appropriate?
4 Are there early warning systems and escalation procedures?

Part of the art of the modern manager is to ensure that chaos is contained and that the company continues along its chosen path. In other words, the manager's job is to stop Murphy's Law (see below) taking root and, if it does, stamp it out immediately. This is easier said than done.

Crisis prediction – some guidelines

The prediction of which events will become crises is as difficult – as outlined earlier – as the science of earthquake prediction. Whilst there may be indicators, it is not foolproof and will never be 100 per cent reliable. Hard and fast definitions are, therefore, difficult. However, there are certain common factors that surround all crises. They should be:

- Simple in concept
- Scientifically complex
- Data-rich
- Slogan-ability
- Open to speculation
- Related to issues.

Simple in concept

The crisis must be simple and capable of being defined as either black or white. This allows sides to be taken, particularly by the media. So for *Brent*

Spar, the issue of sea dumping was bad and recycling of the structure on land (as advocated by Greenpeace) was good. GM foods are bad – we do not know enough about them. Organic foods are good. Nuclear power is bad (even though almost all developed nations use it) as the waste cannot be disposed of; green energy is good. So some members of the Lutheran Church – which boycotted Shell products – did not even know whether it was the North Sea or the North Atlantic the *Spar* was going to. Nor did they need to. The concept was simple: no sea dumping; the science of where it was to be dumped, and the reasons behind it, did not need to be understood.

Scientifically complex

Paradoxically, the science surrounding the crisis must be extremely complex and impenetrable to the ordinary person. This is essential as otherwise people would be able to make reasoned decisions on what is right and what is wrong. So the science surrounding the disposal of the *Brent Spar* was very complex – how many pollutants were on the *Spar* and how much damage would they do? Would the structure, as it sunk to the bottom of the North Atlantic, provide a haven for the sea creatures there? Or would it damage the ecology of the ocean floor? The learned rent-a-quote professors were wheeled out and argued over the heads of the people, confusing the issue further and moving the scientific arguments out of the national debate and into conference rooms and lecture halls.

At a local level, the simple act of building a road, a shop or a housing estate now throws up reams of statistics. Every major new development in the UK requires a Traffic Impact Assessment, which is all but impenetrable except to the consultants who wrote it. In addition, these statistics are capable of interpretation in many ways. By hiding behind a wall of figures, it makes the company look bad. Emotions are what are needed, and what get a response. This is why green groups can quickly take the agenda – the environment is an emotional issue.

Data-rich

Today's corporation makes available more data about its performance than it ever did. This is published by the various agencies and is available to the public. Even confidential information is not safe: leaks of sensitive information are now commonplace. One sure way to get a document noticed and carefully read is to mark it as 'confidential'.

Even before the Internet, we lived in a world that was rich with data albeit slightly less accessible. In the USA, the Freedom of Information Act means that almost all data can be made available to everyone on request. No secrets – just transparency. The major activist groups can spend months trawling through data. It is then presented as 'a major leak of a secret report' in order to increase its media saleability.

ALUMINIUM AND ALZHEIMER'S

Of course, the problem with all data is that when you turn it into information, it can be construed and interpreted in a number of ways. So, for example, in the late 1980s, there was a thought that Alzheimer's might be linked to the intake of aluminium. There were numerous studies that seemed to point that it could be a causal factor.

The environmental groups were quick to latch onto the fact that there were traces of aluminium in tap water and they turned this into a crisis for the water companies in the UK. They used this fact to claim that drinking tap water could lead to the disease. This was at the height of an unpopular privatisation of the water industry in the UK and it got substantial coverage. The result: bottled water companies rubbed their hands in glee as sales got a boost.

As it turned out, the link between aluminium and Alzheimer's is now thought to be highly unlikely. The amount of aluminium in tap water is not even comparable to the dose you might get from, say, wrapping your sandwiches in foil.

Analysis
The point is that, in environmental issues, there is no truth, only data. From this data, one can manufacture, quite legitimately, information, perspectives and assumptions and this can be accepted by people (like those who bought bottled water) as knowledge.

Knowledge is our perception of what the facts are. In today's world, in dealing with environmental and similar issues, there is no reality, just perceptions. These perceptions are what people believe and must be taken into account when dealing with the public. They may not necessarily be correct; however, they cannot be ignored.

Slogan-ability

The crisis must be capable of being summarised in a couple of short words. This is also the essence of good branding: BMW is 'The Ultimate Driving Machine', for Avis – 'We try harder' and so on. So the disposal of nuclear waste is: 'Out of sight, out of mind.' GM foods are 'Frankenstein foods'. *Brent Spar* is akin to dumping a car in the village pond.

Slogans like this are hard to argue with – generally because they have enough truth in them to make them credible, and they have no 'small print' to qualify them. In addition, large organisations – even though they may be brilliant at marketing – are not good at responding to this type of attack. The Law of the Absolute gets in the way (see below). These slogans are hard to counter.

The semantics of science are appalling compared to the semantics of marketing, which is what the green groups exploit. They – like the devil – always have the best tunes. There are 'radioactive dumps' and 'Franken-stein foods'. But is science much better at describing the same things: neither 'repository' nor 'genetically modified organisms' exactly trip off the tongue and sound less palatable. For the media, there is no choice: the words to be used are those that are most understandable (the charitable view) or those that shock most (the cynical view). When trying to explain controversial scientific advances in the mass media, unfortunately those that generate the most understanding and shock are usually the same word.

The Law of the Absolute

There has to be some element of doubt within the debate – which is why scientifically complex and data-rich projects make ideal environmental issues. There is a corollary to the law which says: the more you know, the less you know. So as science advances and more complex instruments are developed that are capable of identifying the presence of even the most minuscule levels of a substance, the more difficult it becomes to proclaim anything safe. More and more, as science makes advances, it throws new light, but it also shows how imperfect our knowledge is. Hence the Law of the Absolute. So, to the question 'Can you categorically assure me that drinking mineral water with tiny traces of benzene will never ever harm me?', the categorical answer of 'no' is not available. The next best answer is not good enough for our first world, health conscious populace. This is powerful and its use by the media is examined later in the book.

Naturally, environmentalists love the Law of the Absolute. It means that there is danger inherent in everything, which they are happy to point out to anyone who will listen, including a grateful media.

Related to issues

As Henry Kissinger said: 'Do not let an issue become a crisis.' Yet that is what usually happens. The crisis may not be dramatic. A scientific report showing that the populations of certain whales were diminishing rapidly led to the campaign to save them. The safety of ocean-going supertankers only became an issue after the crisis of the *Exxon Valdez* in Alaska in the 1980s. By then, the memory of the last disaster, the *Torrey Canyon*, off the south coast of England in 1967 had been forgotten.

Indeed, it could be argued that an issue is not an issue until it either becomes, or has been, a crisis. The nuclear industry is typical of one which went from being a motherhood cause – promising unlimited supplies of electricity which was 'too cheap to meter' – to today where the likelihood of building new nuclear power stations in most western European countries is almost zero. To become such as issue, the industry suffered a number of crises, from Three Mile Island to Chernobyl, radioactive prawns and more.

The stronger the issues, the more likely the industry is to suffer crises. To this day, Shell is suffering the aftermath of *Brent Spar* and 17 years later, in 2004, the chairman resigned in another crisis as oil reserves had been understated. Once a corporation is in crisis mode, it is – like a fast-moving Ferris wheel – difficult to get off.

Murphy's Law

This planning, the practicalities of which are outlined in Section C, is all very well except for one factor that no one can predict – Murphy's Law. One variant of this states: 'Whatever can go wrong, will go wrong.' It is uncanny that when a crisis strikes, it always seems to be at either the time of holidays, weekends or when people are not prepared.

Certainly the active green groups, if they are manufacturing a crisis, will choose their timing with deadly accuracy. For example, when Oxfam wanted to attack Nestlé (see the case study in Chapter 8), it chose the week before Christmas.

There are a number of corollaries to Murphy's Law:

1. 'No one is ever in the right place at the right time.' As noted above, crises do not occur to order, and training (dealt with in Section C) and careful planning are essential. Training must be real and happen unexpectedly, not like the chief executive of one firm we were working with who tried to stop the crisis simulation happening until he was ready.
2. Mini-Murphys will come to the fore. In other words, things and people which generally operate to the highest efficiency seem suddenly to fail.

3. 'Things always get worse before, or indeed if, they get better.' This is the escalation to the second plateau outlined in Chapter 2.

EXXON VALDEZ

On March 24, 1989, shortly after midnight (Murphy's Law), the oil tanker *Exxon Valdez* hit a reef in Alaska, spilling more than 11 million gallons of crude oil – the biggest in the history of the US oil industry. The spill affected the sensitive ecosystem in the area and eventually it was estimated that some 250,000 birds were killed, including around 150 bald eagles, as well as 5,000 otters, 300 seals and 22 killer whales.

Analysis

In the aftermath of the *Exxon Valdez* incident, Congress passed the Oil Pollution Act of 1990, which greatly increased the powers of the authorities to regulate the oil industry.

But the escalation process as predicted by Murphy's Law continued. For a start, Exxon had to pay $1 billion in damages. Then the industry as a whole was hit with a one-off 25 cents per barrel assessment to create a $50 million fund for use in the event of an incident.

And of course when other oil-related incidents – such as *Brent Spar* – arise, the reputation damage to the oil industry accumulates and makes it even more difficult for the industry to defend itself in a crisis. Even when a crisis does not cause much real damage, a company or industry which has crisis-related scars will be more vulnerable.

THE BRAER – THE EXXON VALDEZ THAT NEVER WAS

On January 5, 1993, the engines of the oil tanker *Braer* failed and the tanker ran aground off the Shetlands in Scotland. This could have had a huge impact on the local wildlife. It immediately attracted the world's press who followed events with great interest. Wild speculation abounded – from a number of parties – as to the massive damage that the spill would cause.

Because of the bad weather and high seas, none of the oil could be taken from the tanker. A week after running aground, the *Braer* began to break up and the entire cargo of 600,000 barrels of crude oil spilled into the sea. However, the choppy seas proved to be useful as they stopped a slick from forming on the sea's surface and the spill broke up quickly. The use of dispersants also helped.

Initially, there was talk of another *Exxon Valdez* but, as it turned out, the damage to wildlife was relatively minor, involving about 1,500 seabirds, some farmed salmon and four otters. Ironically two of the otters were killed when they were hit by a TV camera crew, who were covering the spill.

It is interesting to note that the co-owners of the *Brent Spar* were Exxon, who kept a remarkably low profile during the *Spar* crisis. Perhaps it had learned too well the damage that can be inflicted on reputation from the crisis of six years earlier.

EXERCISE: How likely is the organisation to have a crisis?

In effect, this is what this book is about – how to prepare for and then manage a crisis. As noted at the beginning, the basis of predicting a crisis is a difficult one. However, just because it is difficult does not mean that it should not be attempted.

The following chart does not attempt to provide a definitive system or methodology for identifying what might become a crisis. Rather, it is more like an early warning system. Try it with one particular project or aspect of your business or organisation. A rating system has been adopted with the following measures:

5 Yes or Very High or Very Likely

4 Probably or High

3 Average

2 Unlikely or Low

1 No or Very Low or Very Unlikely

Indicators	Key questions	Ratings (out of five)
■ Simple in concept	■ Can this be easily and quickly understood by a non-scientist?	
	■ Does it provide the potential for real danger – not just to humans but to animals and plants also?	
	■ Do those who oppose look simply like the good guys or you look like the bad guys i.e. you are profit-making?	
■ Scientifically complex	■ Is it possible for a mischievous scientist to totally misrepresent this issue?	
	■ Is there seemingly contradictory evidence?	
	■ Is it a new field or an old one under modification?	
■ Data-rich	■ Is there a substantial body of legislation?	
	■ Are there a great many scientific and technical studies?	
	■ Has someone tried to suppress any of this data?	

Indicators	Key questions	Ratings (out of five)
■ Slogan-ability	■ Is there a simple slogan which summarises the argument? (If one exists, the probability is that the issue will be returned to.)	
	■ Is it photogenic? Can it be made so?	
	■ Can it involve children, animals or fauna?	
■ Open to speculation	■ Is it possible to claim that it might kill or badly hurt people, animals or plants – even if this risk is minuscule?	
	■ Is it impossible to give categorical assurances on safety?	
	■ Are there rent-a-quote professors or stakeholders who will speak out against the issue?	
■ Issues prone	■ Has the industry been hit before?	
	■ Is there a siege mentality in the organisation?	
	■ Is there a fear of media, politicians, etc?	
■ Internal issues	■ Has there been a substantial HR-generated change programme (culture)?	
	■ Have processes changed?	
TOTAL	Max: 100	

75–100: Those projects, industries or aspects of industries which score about 75 should definitely have both proper crisis management and issues management programmes in place. Indeed, it is highly likely that they have, as they have been targeted before. The waste disposal, nuclear and chemicals industry and, nowadays, the oil industry will come into this category. However, if the rating is high and there is no history, one should be prepared. This was the situation all industries were in before it became an issue.

50–75: Companies which fall into this rating are less likely to be subject to crises. However, times change and change quickly. It was only 40 short years ago that the nuclear industry was being hailed as the saviour of the planet and that Perrier was the drink of choice in fashionable downtown Hollywood.

25–50: Risk of becoming an issue is much lower here. This is where cattle rearing was before BSE. It looks harmless, it looks safe but, given the right circumstances, it can explode. Again, it was an internal factor – the feeding of sheep carcasses to vegetarian cattle – which saw a multibillion pound industry go into crisis.

20–25: Only the purest of the pure of the environmental groups can achieve this score.

Another useful exercise is to put oneself on the other side of the fence. Assume you are the local action group, the pressure group or whatever and predict how you would react.

Whilst exercises like the one above are useful and help to concentrate minds, all organisations must assume that – sooner or later – they are going to face something which will become an issue. And, almost always, when they eventually realise it is an issue, that is because it is now a crisis. And in any crisis, the best that one can hope for is damage limitation.

For most organisations, this means fairly radical change in the way they approach their communication programmes. In order to do this, most have to change dramatically.

Prediction is imprecise? Yes, but then so is the world. Those who subscribe to chaos theory are well suited to become crisis managers whose motto might be: 'Expect the unexpected and then be really prepared.'

Conclusion

There are often a huge number of divergent factors which lead to a crisis, so prediction is difficult. For example, with *Brent Spar* there was the important meeting of the EEC ministers, an organisation which was trying to find itself as a real campaigning organisation again and, possibly, the complacency of Shell as to the serious impact these events would have.

However, in manufactured crises, those with very good reputations will be less scarred and recover more quickly. Therefore crisis management has a linkage to corporate social responsibility. Therefore it is important to handle issues well, for example in dealing with suppliers, employees (particularly in less well developed countries), corporate citizenship and so on. The company and its brand must reflect this in its tone of voice and the way it handles issues, its honesty and openness and transparency in dealing with the media, politicians and others and a generous corporate giving scheme.

In other words, a company which handles issues well will be less prone to crises and will recover more quickly from them. That is not to say that either Shell or Monsanto had poor CSR credentials; even the strongest can be hurt by a carefully and powerfully orchestrated campaign such as that mounted by Greenpeace in these two cases.

CHAPTER 4

Why Managing a Crisis Matters

A badly managed crisis can severely damage a company, its reputation and its brand. Handle it badly and one risks losing the company; handle it well and your reputation is enhanced, sales increase and the brand is stronger than ever. As noted in the Introduction, Johnson & Johnson reacted promptly and unequivocally in withdrawing Tylenol when the analgesic was threatened by a blackmailer. And that is how Nike, the sports goods manufacturer, reacted when it was faced with a problem.

NIKE AND GLOBALISATION

Nike is at the forefront of what most people understand as globalisation. It is a brand that reaches across the world but ultimately encapsulates the value system of its country of origin, the USA. The company's trainers are fashionable items bought by those in the west and, whenever possible, by those in the developing world. It is a symbol of aspiration in many countries.

A storm, however, was whipped up following one of the company's designs for a new Nike Air trainer in 1997. On the back of the shoe, Nike had designed what looked to the untrained western eye like an image resembling flames burning. That was to the western eye. However, complaints came flooding in when Muslims claimed that the image was close to the Arab script for Allah.

Nike's response was as quick as it was unequivocal. Instead of questioning whether in fact there was any justification for these claims, Nike acted in a way which suggested it was sympathetic to the sensitivities of others. Nike immediately recalled over 38,000 pairs of the trainers. The company also pulled a clever PR stunt to show just how much it cared by offering to pay for the construction of playgrounds for Muslim families.

Analysis
The crisis dissipated as soon as it had arrived. Certainly, there was a cost in recalling thousands of trainers. But it was a fraction of the cost of fighting an unwinnable battle.

Nike appeared as though there was absolutely no doubt it had ever intended to offend the Muslim population and that it was willing to offer a kind of peace offering. The result: the crisis passed quickly and the Nike brand went unscarred.

Looking at Nike on the crisis curve, it is clear that at the first warning (point B) it reacted quickly.

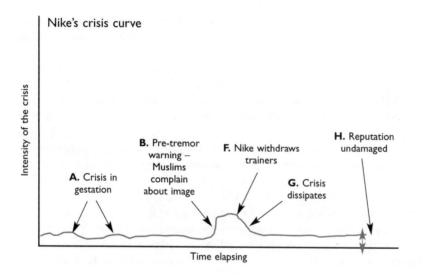

Nike's crisis curve

In simple terms, it is worth repeating the rules for managing a crisis:

1. Look carefully at the signals. What is the worst-case scenario? – that is probably what you are heading for.
2. Make sure immediate costs to possible brand damage are in perspective.
3. Don't rush – make a rational decision in good time.
4. Overcompensate – in response to criticism, be the big man and make the big gesture. This can save time and pain later on.
5. Things will get worse before they get better, so the ostrich syndrome – hoping it will go away – is not an option. It is here to stay.

Both Johnson & Johnson and Nike were quick to react and their reputations were enhanced. Sales improved and the organisations got on with their businesses. Perrier was not so lucky.

THE BUBBLE BURSTS

The world famous Perrier drink is iconoclastic. It has long been associated with a refined taste and was hugely popular with yuppies in the 1980s and 90s. It could do no wrong – it was the epitome of a natural drink coming from deep within the earth where, as it said on the label, it was naturally carbonated. Ideal for the generation who saw their bodies as temples. The drink's traditional markets in Europe had widened and now it was hugely popular in North America as well.

In 1990, scientists had noticed that there were tiny amounts of benzene in the water. These amounts were rising and still the management ignored the warnings. This is not unreasonable; anyone who works in a chemistry laboratory will be familiar with this compound which is a fundamental chemical tool.

Despite the label, what most people did not know was that the Perrier water and the gas that carbonated it did not come from the same underground sources. They came from different sources and were mixed together at the surface. It was here that the contamination had seemed to occur. Perrier did nothing. It ignored the pre-tremor warning.

But American health regulations are tight and, soon after, North Carolina health regulators claimed they had found the chemical benzene in bottles of Perrier. Naturally the general public was not particularly aware of what this meant, but it sounded scary. The fear of the unknown is always great. It leads to speculation, claim and counterclaim. Anxiety levels rose, stimulated by the media's coverage of the story. Perrier was now at point C – the point of no return – the arrow had left the bow; it could not be recalled.

Despite this warning, Perrier took a half-hearted approach to solving the problem. Rather than going for a total recall, as Johnson & Johnson and Nike did, it went for a partial recall as it believed the problem to be a small one, isolated to one or two cases. It decided to withdraw only a limited number of bottles, specifically from the North American market. The company tried to play down the importance of the benzene – despite claims that the chemical was carcinogenic. In the media, it played down the importance of the story and tried to reduce its financial exposure by recalling more bottles.

However, in the event of trying to prevent a crisis, Source Perrier ensured that was exactly what was going to happen. When the news came through that benzene had also been found in Europe, urgent action was required to recall all bottles – worldwide.

Although Source Perrier had now done the necessary, it had effectively been forced into doing so. The company had seemed arrogant and unresponsive – recklessly disregarding the health of millions of its customers. The media characteristically pulled no punches. Perrier bore the brunt of continued negative publicity.

By 1995 sales of the bottled water in America had shrunk by 50 per cent compared to 1989. Source Perrier suffered further ignominy in 1990 when it was forced to ditch its slogan 'naturally sparkling' after the benzene incident alerted officials to the company's carbonating process which was now seen to be not at all natural.

It later became clear that the levels of benzene found in the drink were virtually negligible. To put it into context, a pack of cigarettes has 2000 times the level of that found in Perrier bottles. The company has survived the incident, but sales of the drink have never fully recovered. With proper management of the crisis, Source Perrier would not have had to endure such a media attack.

Perrier was damaged irreparably and now the company is part of the Nestlé Group who have worked hard and successfully to re-establish what was, after all, a reputable and sound brand.

Analysis

Still, the lesson is a salutary one: getting your crisis management wrong means you are in a weak position to control the crisis when it breaks. This is serious and in the worst cases, like Perrier, you lose the company. Perrier's crisis curve is shown below.

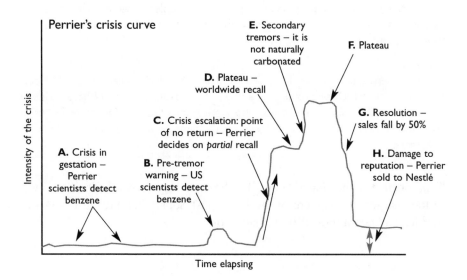

Perrier's crisis curve

Intensity of the crisis

A. Crisis in gestation – Perrier scientists detect benzene

B. Pre-tremor warning – US scientists detect benzene

C. Crisis escalation: point of no return – Perrier decides on *partial* recall

D. Plateau – worldwide recall

E. Secondary tremors – it is not naturally carbonated

F. Plateau

G. Resolution – sales fall by 50%

H. Damage to reputation – Perrier sold to Nestlé

Time elapsing

No room for error

In a crisis, the room to manoeuvre is effectively nil. You have been accused, therefore you must be guilty. This is extremely unfair, but this is the hand with which you must play.

ANTHRAX IN THE POST

After the events of September 11 2001, America was on a state of heightened alert to the threat of terrorist activity. The nation reacted with horror when reports were issued that anthrax had been sent to government officials in the post.

The media whipped up a frenzy, generating increasingly doom-laden stories for an eager public to digest who feared that they could be next to receive a package coated in the deadly virus. The panic was tangible.

The US Postal Service (USPS) acted quickly to try to prevent a further escalation of the situation. The USPS quickly positioned itself as a champion of the people. It sent 145 million homes throughout the country a card which advised people on what to do to avoid being exposed to any anthrax which may have been concealed in their mail. This card also emphasised the company's concern for the wellbeing of the American people.

It read: 'The USPS places the highest priority on the safety of our customers and employees and the security of the mail.' In addition USPS took other measures to ensure that the public had every possible way of finding out the truth of the situation, for example a website to offer further advice was set up and regularly updated.

By ensuring that it appeared to be responsive to people's concerns, USPS distanced itself from being the carrier of the anthrax virus and instead repositioned itself as part of the war against terror.

Analysis

Call it an overreaction to send 145 million postcards, but that is what is needed. Under-reaction – the ostrich syndrome – is a recipe for disaster and would have seriously damaged the USPS. Of course, it was also a great advertisement for the mail – using your own service to warn of the dangers that the same service might bring in the form of anthrax.

Total openness and transparency are the only way forward. This is how – in the charged atmosphere of the US – post September 11, the US Postal Service handled a most difficult situation.

SECTION B

The Organisation and its Universe

CHAPTER 5

Organisations and their Leadership

When a company is in a crisis, it tends to become defensive and inward-looking. This is not surprising – it is the caveman response. In pre-historic times, people would retreat into their caves for safety, to have three solid walls around them at the time of attack. In medieval times, people pulled up the drawbridge as the same response and tried to defend against the attackers. Therefore most crisis management procedures draw only on internal resources. As outlined in the second half of this book, good crisis management procedures are absolutely essential, but organisations are very slow to shout 'help'. So, for example, in the *Brent Spar* case, Shell did not call on Exxon even though it was a 50 per cent owner of the installation. Nor did Monsanto call on those professors who had done numerous studies on the safety of GM foods.

The reasons for going alone are many, but they can include fear, embarrassment and arrogance.

Fear

There is a strong control fixation within organisations which, in most cases, rightly tries to control messages and how they are disseminated. There is a real concern that if others are allowed to defend the company, they may not do so as well or as robustly. As any army general will attest, however, alliances are absolutely essential in fighting a war. In both world wars, the European alliances worked hard to encourage a reluctant United States to enter the war. In World War I, it took the sinking of the civilian ship *The Lusitania* to bring the US into the war and in World War II, it took Pearl Harbour. The European nations, however, particularly Britain, recognised the need for an alliance if the war was to be won.

Similarly in a crisis, an organisation must draw on resources other than its own if it is to win the battle in the long term.

Embarrassment

Corporations in particular tend to have a very strong image which they are careful to cultivate for certain audiences, particularly the financial community. Weakness does not look good for the management who have to portray that they are following a carefully thought-out strategy. Therefore, it can be embarrassing if they are seen to seek help from other organisations, particularly when their antagonists are perceived to be a small NGO.

Arrogance

This is the most dangerous of all human characteristics. At the best of times, most of us are not as good as we think we are and in a crisis, none of us are. Arrogance is the equivalent of putting on a blindfold and running along a cliff path.

The legal department

Large organisations are very cautious in a crisis. It is hard to do much else when you are in a cave. It is important that all statements are carefully cleared and management prepared in advance.

ELECTRICITY TOO CHEAP TO METER

In the 1950s, at the beginning of the nuclear era when atomic power was just emerging, it seemed as if it was a panacea for the world's energy needs. There was a lot of optimism throughout the world following the war a decade earlier.

Nor were there the environmental and safety concerns which exist today and which are thousands of times more rigorous than they were then. At that time, an American scientist said that one day nuclear power would be so cheap, it would be too cheap to meter. In other words, the economic cost of a meter would not make sense because the power itself would be so inexpensive.

Unfortunately, it has still not come to fruition and today nuclear power is extremely expensive, mainly because of safety and environmental concerns which are rightly tackled by the industry. However, this statement 'too cheap to meter' is used again and again by NGOs who want to attack the industry. It is put forward as overoptimism, as trying to spin the truth or as a plain lie. It is extremely difficult to defend.

Analysis

An organisation needs to be careful what it says about its activities, whether it is in crisis or not. Unfortunately, a crisis can lead to injudicious statements which can never be withdrawn and which will haunt the organisation and its reputation for ever.

Often what emerges from an organisation during a crisis is late and with little content. This is not very media or stakeholder friendly. The problems are that the legal department – for good reasons – wants to ensure that the organisation does not expose itself during a crisis. As one cynic said, the default position of all lawyers is to say nothing.

Tone of voice

In a crisis, organisations tend to adopt one of three tones of voice, defensive, aggressive and business as usual.

Defensive
This is the caveman response and it can look very weak. The organisation is under attack – is in crisis – and yet nothing is heard. This gives the impression of a cover-up, incompetence or worse.

Aggressive
This is based on the principle that attack is the best form of defence. Unfortunately, when an organisation is in crisis, attack is not appropriate. At best it can look uncaring, at worst it can look arrogant. A typical example of an aggressive response could be during an environmental crisis when the organisation says: 'Certainly there seem to have been a number of fish killed in this incident; however, the source of the pollution has been cleared up and we believe that we have worked extremely hard to mitigate the damage. In fact, without our quick and appropriate action, the damage could have been much worse'. This aggressive response is inappropriate and is the equivalent of a shrug of the shoulders – the 'so-what' response.

Business as usual
This is a form of denial which is best represented by the phrase: 'Crisis, what crisis?' Even though you may not be in crisis, to be accused of being in crisis is to be in crisis.

PARMALAT

The downfall of this Italian food and dairy company is an example of how businesses can face bankruptcy by both self- and public deception.

Parmalat is one of Italy's best known businesses. The company's core product, long-life milk, is ubiquitous in Mediterranean countries and throughout the world. Despite its success, the company was declared officially insolvent at the end of 2003. So how did this happen?

The troubles began when Parmalat was unable to account for a stray €4 billion. The company said that some 38 per cent of its assets were held in an offshore bank account in the Cayman Islands. However, it soon became clear that the company was unable to produce this cash, that the account was in fact a fiction. Following this discovery, the ensuing investigation uncovered that managers had invented assets to offset over €14 billion in liabilities and falsified accounts over a 15-year period.

The final figure of debt then was much higher than the original €4 billion. Parmalat, once found out, failed to reveal the extent to which it was in trouble. This had the effect of compounding the crisis for the company. It was not the amount of debt that was the problem, but the manner in which Parmalat attempted to cover it up. All confidence in the company had been slashed.

After these events, key figureheads of the company were dragged into the public eye and unceremoniously prosecuted for their corporate crime. Former Chief Executive Calisto Tanzi, his son Stefano and brother Giovanni, former Chief Financial Officer Fausto Tonna and 16 other individuals were all taken to court to face charges.

Analysis

Parmalat committed the worst of sins in crisis management. By not admitting to the truth, the company became further embroiled.

The tone of voice should be modest but firm, drawing on the lifebelt statements outlined in Chapter 15. It must leave all triumphalism behind. Nor is it the time for corporate breast-beating of any sort. For example, statements such as 'we have a very proud environmental record and have won a number of awards for our work' are a waste of time. People do not want to know the corporate PR. In fact, in a crisis, it is best if you do not believe any of your own PR.

The role of the chief executive

In Section C of the book, details of the practicalities of setting up a crisis management team are explained. However, there is an important player outside the team, who will also have an important role in the crisis process.

In essence, there are three broad roles which the chief executive of an organisation can take during a crisis:

1. Lead from the front and take total control of the crisis
2. Leave the management of the crisis to the crisis management team
3. A combination of the above – poolside management.

Lead from the front

Most chief executives tend to gravitate towards this position. After all, their organisation is under fierce attack and it is only right that the general of the army is seen to be on a white steed, sword in hand, defending it to the death. There are, unfortunately, a number of problems with this position:

- *It leaves the leader of the organisation fully exposed.* Certainly, many famous generals such as Napoleon at the Arcole Bridge, who ran into a hail of bullets, or Wellington at the Battle of Waterloo led successfully from the front. However, these people are rare and if the leader is attacked and loses his/her position, then this leaves the organisation highly vulnerable. For example, in 2003 Shell was in crisis over under-statement of its oil reserves. The chief executive was brought into the fray and promptly lost his job. This was very damaging for Shell.

- *There is still an organisation to run.* Although the crisis, because of its intensity and short time burst, seems to be overwhelming and the organisation of a response and nothing else seems to be of any impor- tance, there is still a corporation which needs management. (This is covered in detail in Chapter 19 on business continuity.) This is partic- ularly so during a crisis, when those who are not directly involved can feel isolated. Even during the most intense crisis, however, there is still a certain amount of 'business as usual'. Even at the height of the *Brent Spar* incident – when Shell stations in Germany were being fire- bombed – there was still a huge multinational organisation selling its products throughout the world.

- *Time for training.* Ask most chief executives if they can take five or six working days out of their year, for what many see as a game, albeit an important game, but a game all the same. They will answer they have no time for games. The result is that they do not have a full under- standing of how a crisis management team works. This is extremely dangerous if they are to lead it, or take a key role in its organisation.

For these reasons, it is probably best if the chief executive does not lead the crisis management team because as the chief executive of the company, he is running it as a totality rather than one specific project – the crisis.

Leave it to the crisis management team

In this scenario, the chief executive does not involve himself or herself directly in the crisis management team. This is by far the best and most preferred option. It does not mean that the chief executive has no part or is not aware of what is happening within the crisis, but he or she is not an active part of the management team. Of course, there is a role for the chief executive and this is outlined below.

Poolside management

This is the situation where the chief executive has agreed that he/she will not be a part of the crisis management team. However, like a moth to a flame, he/she is drawn to the crisis; as has been pointed out in other parts of the book – a crisis is fun. It brings out all the thrills of the chase. Now the chief executive is drawn magnetically and begins to offer direction. Because it is the chief executive, this direction is extremely difficult to resist. In fact, in many companies it can be career-limiting to countermand the orders of the chief executive.

This situation is exacerbated when the chief executive is remote from the crisis management team and the crisis management room. Numerous telephone calls come in, generally after each news bulletin, offering advice, comfort and threats.

The ideal role for the chief executive

There is a key role that the chief executive can take and, given that we do not live in a perfect or ideal world, this *must* be agreed in advance. This means it is written down within the procedures and then explained carefully in writing to the chief executive what his/her role will be. Some time should be taken over this explanation. Ideally, a couple of hours should be taken to explain the crisis management procedures and the chief executive's role within it.

If this is not done in advance, there is a real problem. Trying to explain the CEO's role in the middle of a crisis is difficult, in fact it is another crisis.

So what then is the role of the chief executive? The following case is an excellent illustration of how the role can work.

THE BRITISH MIDLAND CRASH

In 1989, an internal British Midland flight from London crashed near Birmingham. A number of people were killed and many were injured. As is common with many crises, it happened on a Sunday evening.

British Midland had good crisis management procedures in place and the crisis management team was assembled. Sir Michael Bishop, the chief executive, even though it was a Sunday night/early Monday, went to the crash site. Here he sympathised with victims and their relatives. He said that the company would do all in its power to find out what had gone wrong and would look to compensate those people who had been affected. Obviously, this was all captured by the media and presented the company as being very customer-focused and sympathetic.

Certainly Sir Michael spoke to the media as he was trained to do, but did not involve himself in any of the technical aspects of the crisis, for example what had gone wrong. These questions can easily be batted back well with the 'lifebelt' statement of: 'We will need to conduct a full investigation and no doubt the results of this will be made fully public in due course. In the meantime, our thoughts must be with the family and friends.'

Analysis

This friendly and sympathetic approach was important to protect British Midland's reputation. It is also an ideal role for the chief executive. It is seen to be leading from the front, while not actually being on the front line which is the crisis management centre. Long term, the crash did little damage to British Midlands' reputation and sales rose.

Conclusion

An organisation in crisis can turn inward-looking and defensive. Sometimes it will not look to third party advocates (TPAs) and will struggle on as a lone fighter. This is a mistake. A well-trained and articulate chief executive has a key role in the crisis, but not in managing it. Well deployed, the CEO can almost become a key TPA for the company.

CHAPTER 6

The Media in a Crisis

By far one of the most informative books in the world is your local telephone directory. Usually it is totally accurate and is full of useful information. It has only one problem: it is boring. People – unless they are very bored – do not read telephone books.

Look at your newspaper. What are the stories (note that word – we will come back to it) that it carries? In essence, they fall into two broad categories:

- information
- entertainment.

The media as entertainer

Certainly most journalists would like to think – and many would insist – that they are in the information business. And indeed some are. But most, by far, are also – and many predominantly – in the entertainment business. If you do not believe this, then stop at your local newspaper kiosk on the way home and buy any of the many publications which feature an almost exclusive diet of sex, violence and sport. In other words, entertainment and conflict. And a crisis is real conflict.

Conflict is entertaining – that is why we enjoy sport. It is also why some of us enjoy blood sports such as fox-hunting.

And a crisis is sport. It is entertaining to watch a great big corporation wriggling on the end of a hook, whilst the world throws rotten tomatoes at it.

DOW CORNING

Dow Corning, the silicone implant company, was at the forefront of the plastic surgery business. If you lived in Hollywood, you would have seen its 'products' every day, as pneumatic starlets and ordinary folk alike graced the boulevards of tinsel town. As with most things Californian, however, it made its way into the lives of people all over the world.

The bubble soon burst after it was revealed that each implant was a potential time bomb waiting to explode. The dangers of the silicone leaking and the damage this would cause, once it was apparent, sounded the death knell for the company.

The company's nemesis was hastened by a media storm. Journalists were extremely happy to report such a story with its sexual overtones and they took delight in highlighting the countless law suits filed against the company. Dow Corning's reaction, however, was a classic example of what not to do in a crisis situation.

The company reacted by acting as if the problem didn't exist. It retreated into its offices hoping that, by keeping its head in the sand, the whole thing would blow over. This was a fateful miscalculation. The story had such obvious selling power in the media that there was little chance of the coverage calming down. Coupled with this, as the profile of the story grew and grew, more and more women came forward, expressing either concern or evidence of harm caused by their leaking implants. The effect was that the crisis became almost self-perpetuating.

This all had the effect of making Dow Corning look as though it was hiding the truth from the public – many in the media concluded that it was. Dow Corning was accused of being deceptive and lying to its customers.

Although Dow Corning employed all the resources at its disposal, it was failing to win the battle. This is something which Dow Corning itself soon recognised. The management lamented: 'The message agenda had been led for far too long by journalists, special interest groups and medical commentators often lacking solid scientific evidence.'

Analysis
As we have seen before, scientific evidence is no substitute for rumour, scaremongering and anxiety. This is much more interesting and easy for the layman to understand. Swift action to make the public aware of the issues was needed. Ideally, this should have been led by third party advocates. It was not to be. Unfortunately the company reacted too late. When it began to become more open, a sceptical media came to the conclusion that it had only done so because its hand was forced. Its message was lost in the fog of hysteria and accusations of cover-ups.

The media also loves an underdog, just as in a football match all the neutral supporters tend to support the weaker team – the giant killer. Journalists often see themselves as consumer champions and so have no difficulty in siding against the big corporation in a crisis. After all, it is this journalistic attitude that spawned various 'doorstepping' investigative programmes across the world, each looking for that big story that could make a career.

Today, even the most staid of news programmes looks for entertainment value; they have no choice; the battle for readers, listeners and viewers is a fierce one. News, for the most part, is intrinsically boring. People say they find politics 'boring' and faraway wars in little known countries have little impact or attraction for the viewing public in the race for ratings. However, celebrity magazines are news, so why do we think one superstar's new boyfriend is more important than the future of a country? Is it because – simply – it is easier to understand?

In a crisis, we often have the basis of a Hollywood movie. The good guys, the underdogs – in the shape of the eco-warriors, local residents or the general public, guardians of all that is good – and the bad guys, the corporation, supported by heavies in the form of the police and so on.

Media want to present news and ideally this information should also be entertaining. However, if the company in crisis helps the entertainment value, then they can assured of high media attention – little of which will be positive.

News only becomes interesting when it becomes entertaining. That is the role of the media, and also recognised by NGOs. Entertainment comes in many forms, but by far the two best components remain those that are

well recognised in Hollywood: sex and violence. *Brent Spar* was violence at its Hollywood best. We all knew no one would be killed, there was a great big baddie in the shape of Shell and the good guys in the shape of Greenpeace. No wonder the BBC and the rest were led by the noses to transmit it: this was high-grade entertainment.

A mantra for the modern media might be:

> Entertain them and you can tell them anything, bore them and you can tell them nothing.

Look at newspapers from around the turn of the century (opposite page, left). They had lots of close type and were very information-intensive. Compare them with today's newspapers with their sensational headlines and photos (opposite page, right). The shift from information to entertainment – known in the trade as 'dumbing down' – has gathered pace as time has passed.

The role of the media in a crisis

People have a low level of trust in the media. According to the 1998 British Social Attitude Survey, quoted in the *UK Press Gazette*, only 15 per cent of the population trust the country's journalists to pursue the truth. In addition, people have little or no respect for journalists, rating them just above estate agents.

What then is the problem? Why not ignore the media? After all, if no one believes or trusts the media, why should any organisation care about it? The answer is a fairly simple one and was first formulated by Chen in 1963 in the book *The Press and Foreign Policy*:

> The press may not be successful much of the time in telling people what to think, but it is stunningly successful in telling its readers what to think *about*.

So people expect the media to be inaccurate, they do not expect even to read the truth in their newspapers, so why is the media well read and heeded in these circumstances?

It is this ability to act as a spotlight that gives the media such power. And not only is it a spotlight, it is also a magnifying glass. It is fairly well accepted in most corporate cultures that the person who controls the agenda and the minutes is in a powerful position. This is exactly where the media sits. It can set the agenda and then write the minutes.

And reading those minutes in a crisis are the politicians, the regulators and other media, in essence, those people who can deliver – or revoke your licence to operate (see Chapter 9). Although they may not take their opinions from the media, and filter out the wilder speculation, they are still influenced by what they see, hear and read. The fact that they are taking the time (precious as it is) to actually pay attention to the media means they have an investment in the media. They would not be reading the newspaper if they did not want something from it. Therefore the media cannot be ignored.

The truth – the first casualty in a crisis

During the *Brent Spar* case, the media took Greenpeace's word as being gospel. Even when it miscalculated the amount of toxic substance on the platform by many orders of magnitude – and had to apologise to Shell – these inaccuracies were faithfully broadcast by an entertainment-hungry media.

Greenpeace offered no apologies for the inaccuracies in its advertising. When asked if it was being naughty in its interpretation of the facts, the Greenpeace spokesman said: 'If you are a political pressure group, you have to be a bit naughty.'

So whilst the media has a duty to inform, this will always be over-ridden by the instinct for survival. And these survival instincts are fuelled by more readers, listeners and viewers. And information alone will not bring them in.

Ironically, the highest information quotient is often found in the adver-tising. Advertising, unlike the editorial, is subject to fairly stringent regula-tion. The editorial content is not. Whereas it may not be fair for journalists to speculate, there is little to stop them getting speculation from other sources. There is no compunction on those who speculate to be accurate. In fact, in many cases, it is against their interest to be accurate, as wild and unfounded speculation is often far more entertaining.

However, this drive to entertain can have a frightening effect on the truth. In newspaper offices the talk is not of 'news' or 'facts', but of 'stories'. This is a strong and tacit acceptance that the media has a role to play in 'telling a story'. In fact, in the cynical world of newspapers, there is an adage which says:'Never let the facts get in the way of a good story.'

In a court of law, witnesses are asked to swear that they will tell the 'truth, the whole truth and nothing but the truth'. So what is the difference between the 'truth', the 'whole truth' and 'nothing but the truth'? Why are there three elements? In an adversarial system of justice such as the American or British one, the prosecution (the state) can intentionally hide pieces of evidence which would be beneficial to the defendant, but detrimental to the prosecution case. Is this the 'whole truth'?

By definition, no piece of news can be completely accurate. Editors are, after all, editors. But editing, by its very definition, distorts the truth, even if it is done with the best intention and in an unbiased way. Ironically, the fewer words that a medium has to play with, the more accurate the story is likely to be. So, for example, a 30-minute television news bulletin may contain 15 separate news items and between 2000 and 3000 words. This is about one page on a fairly dense broadsheet like the *New York Times*, but covering only three or four stories.

Therefore, editors have a very difficult job. They have to select the facts and assemble them in such a way as to present what they believe is as complete a picture as possible which represents the truth.

The problem in a crisis is that facts are often hard to come by. But the media cannot tolerate a vacuum – there are hectares of newsprint to be filled, hours of broadcasting. If the facts are not available, then speculation will have to do.

However, journalists are generally fairly moral and ethical people. Certainly, some will speculate off their own bat, but others will look for someone 'to stand the story up'. This is where pundits and experts come in. To become an expert is fairly easy: just put the title 'doctor' or 'professor' in front of your name and you are 90 per cent there. You could also start up your own organisation; after all, in this technologically advanced world, we all have access to the web, email and a vast new world of members.

The activist groups are often ready and willing to come forward as experts in a crisis. After all, they are looking for the publicity that will attract new members.

Meantime, the organisation at the heart of the crisis is still trying to get a statement cleared. In the Nestlé case in Ethiopia, outlined in Chapter 8, it took five days to get a media statement. Meantime, Oxfam had a field day. And when the media statement did appear, it was on December 27 when much of the world was comatosely recovering from Christmas.

The balancing comment

Ever since the penny dreadfuls of Victorian times, readers of newspapers have liked to be shocked, in much the same way as people like horror

films. However, there is a line and newspaper editors have to be careful
not to transgress it.

But surely there must be balance. Of course, it is called the 'balancing
comment'. When the reporter has written the shock-horror story, the
organisation is then approached for a comment 'to balance out the piece.'
Even if the company manages to say something strong and sensible or
even manages to refute totally the story as a tissue of lies, this will appear
at the very bottom of the story.

Of course, reporters and editors are aware that there is a huge decay
curve in how newspaper stories are read. Nearly everyone reads the headlines, but by the time they get to the balancing comment, only a tiny
proportion of the readers remains. The headline itself is 90 per cent of the
impact and if the subeditor has any qualms about one, such as 'Local Firm
Will Wipe Out Last of the Newts', it is just put into quotation marks – after
all the green group did say it.

In the *Brent Spar* incident, Greenpeace initially accused Shell of
wanting to dump the platform in the North Sea. In fact, it was the North
Atlantic – a totally different stretch of water. A Greenpeace spokesperson
discounted this as being immaterial – it's the principle that counts. This, of
course, is the same organisation that demands meticulous accuracy from
all those it attacks.

Dealing positively with the media

So what can a large organisation do? The response of most is based on
classical public relations. However, the problem with classical PR is that it
is based on consumerism. Here the customer is willing to buy (or at least is
wanting to consider buying) the product. In crisis communications, the
opposite is true. There is antagonism towards the company.

Compare, for example, buying a new car and having a chemical
factory explode in your village. In the first case, you are happy to read
about the model you wish to buy: in fact, the more glowing the press
reports, the more reassured you are about your buying decision. In the case
of the factory, you want to believe everything that is bad. And you definitely will not believe anything the promoting organisation wishes to tell
you about. They would say that, wouldn't they?

However, the media – as Greenpeace found out – can be also manipu-
lated for the company's own ends. It means that one has to be fleet (dead-
lines are always tight) and willing to think laterally. Here's how the Allied
Irish Bank (AIB) handled what could have become a Barings Bank/Nick

Leeson story. Barings was eventually sold to ING Bank of the Netherlands for £1. AIB was luckier, or was it just better prepared?

AIB BANK

The Allied Irish Bank is Ireland's biggest banking and financial services organisation. The company was formed in 1966 and grew from humble beginnings into a multinational corporation employing 31,000 people in more than 1000 offices.

In early 2002, the company was thrown into crisis when it was reported that one of its traders had defrauded it of $750 million.

Almost as soon the news reached the press, John Rusnak, the rogue trader in question, was labelled as the next Nick Leeson. This was bad news indeed for AIB. Leeson famously brought about the collapse of Barings Bank by running up £830 million in losses on unauthorised derivatives trades. The implication was there for all to see.

The situation threatened to spiral out of control as it appeared that Mr Rusnak had disappeared. Sensing a story with Hollywood blockbuster qualities, the media concluded that he was on the run. Speculation was rife and the media was hooked.

The bank called a crisis meeting to discuss quite how it could have got into this situation. Almost at the same time, AIB received some fortunate news: Mr Rusnak had spoken to the FBI. It transpired that he was not on the run, after all, but was visiting family in Baltimore.

Seizing on this opportunity, the bank took the initiative to distance itself from comparisons to Nick Leeson and Barings Bank. The bank immediately briefed the press. First it explained the situation with Mr Rusnak and, more importantly, it acted to quell rumours that as a result the company would go under. AIB informed the watching public that the financial blow it had taken was not on anything like the same scale as that which befell Barings Bank.

Analysis
In a master stroke, AIB issued a good news story. The bank told journalists that the figures showed that, despite the loss, the company would still report a profit for the year.

Effectively, the stories of collapse and the damaging prospect of a prolonged manhunt for Rusnak were killed in an instant. Not quite crisis averted, but certainly crisis curtailed.

Conclusion

In a crisis, you have no choice but to handle the media. It must be done, and the practicalities are outlined in Section C. However, what most organisations fail to do – Greenpeace being an honourable exception – is to invoke the power of third party advocates. How TPAs can be used in a crisis is covered in Chapter 11.

CHAPTER 7

The Politicians and Regulators

When asked what goes wrong in politics, the former British prime minister, Harold Macmillan, said: 'Events, dear boy, events.'

A crisis is certainly an event. Because, as Macmillan said, it is events which make things go wrong, politicians tend, unless they are drawn in, to steer well clear of crises. Because politicians are the fountainhead of power, those who are attacking the corporation (often the pressure groups) try hard to embroil the politicians in the crisis. Of course, if the politicians are embroiled, it is all the more exciting for the media which, in turn, further escalates the intensity of the crisis.

Characteristics of a politician

In order to understand the role of politicians in a crisis, it is important to understand the nature of the beast. Whilst stereotyping is always dangerous, there are two characteristics which are common to most politicians: altruism and ego.

Altruism

Most politicians have a strong sense of duty. One of the reasons they go into what is a tough and often unrewarding profession is to 'serve their communities'. Publicly, they would present a strong sense of duty and loyalty to that community. If the community is attacked, as it is often perceived to be during a crisis, then they will jump to the defence of that community. This is to be expected and should be planned for.

COKE WASN'T IT

Coca-Cola is one of the most ubiquitous of global brands – it seems it can be bought on any corner of any foreign land.

A company like this can rely on the strength of its brand to see it through most things. However, complacency in a crisis is a dangerous thing indeed. In 1999, Coke suffered a serious setback. It did not threaten the survival of the company – that would require a seismic shift in the public's attitude – but it did seriously damage the company's reputation and dent its stock market value.

On June 14 1999, the Belgian Government banned the sale of Coca-Cola. A month earlier 43 school children had complained of nausea and vomiting after drinking it. Coco-Cola ignored this and carried on with business as usual. As the cases grew, however, the company began to apportion blame elsewhere. It refused to accept responsibility for the ill health of customers. It also refused to stop production.

As the weeks progressed, the evidence was mounting. More than 250 people had reported feeling ill after drinking Coke. The company, however, remained defensive and the media began to attack. Coca-Cola's stock plummeted.

While it continued to deny any connection, the Belgian Government took action to ban the drink. Coca-Cola issued a statement confirming that the product had been cont-aminated, but that it would only cause minor discomfort to those who drank it. The government and the people of Belgium had expected a different response. They were looking for apologies, explanations and compensation. Coca-Cola refused to act.

The panic spread. Governments in three other European countries ordered that Coke be recalled from the shelves.

In July, Coca-Cola decided that it would apologise – but this apology was made primarily to shareholders in the form of a letter. Even in this letter the apology was not complete. Douglas Ivestor, chairman of Coca-Cola, blamed what he called 'bad' carbon dioxide for the problems. Later this was challenged by scientists. Whatever the cause, the media was cynical and unimpressed by this belated response. Coca-Cola also tried the tactic of giving away millions of drinks to the Belgian population. However, this also fell flat.

Analysis

Politicians will steer clear of a crisis for as long as possible. After all, when there is mud flying, they don't want it to stick on them. However, there comes a time when politicians must step in to defend the communities they represent. A company should act long before this happens. In the end, Coca-Cola had to launch a huge public relations exercise to try to regain its customers.

Ego

The world of politics is not one for shy, modest or retiring individuals. Whereas most politicians would like to give the impression that they have been forced to take up office, exactly the opposite is true. They will often present this dilemma with quotes such as: 'If there are those in my party who would force me to allow my name to go forward, then of course I will bend to the wishes of the party if it should believe that this is in the best interests of my constituents and my country.'

To be a successful politician, one needs huge amounts of self-belief and self-confidence. Ambition, it goes without saying, is another absolute prerequisite. Obviously, as ambition can often be perceived as naked greed for power, politicians are careful to hide it beneath a veneer of modesty. Even the mildest, self-effacing politicians need a high level of ambition if they are to be in any way successful.

The politician in a crisis

When a crisis breaks, politicians, and again this has been stereotypical, have two simple choices: either get involved or not. For most people, in the vicinity of a lab explosion, the natural reaction is to duck and run for cover. This is also the natural reaction of the politician.

However, outside forces may not allow that actuality to occur.

AUSTRALIAN ASYLUM SEEKER BOAT

Saving lives at sea must always rank ahead of politics.

This quote is from Arne Rinnan, the Norwegian boat captain who rescued 438 refugees stranded about 75 nautical miles north of Christmas Island. He had received a general call from the Australian Rescue Coordination Centre (RCC) that the *Palapa* (the refugees' ship) was stranded and in a bad condition and that any nearby vessel's assistance was required. Rinnan's ship, the MS *Tampa*, was the closest and rescued all the refugees. Rinnan was originally due in Singapore and intended to continue on this route. However, the asylum seekers became agitated at this, threatening various actions, including jumping overboard. The captain decided to sail for the Australian Christmas Islands instead.

Now the crisis really began.

Upon approaching the islands, the captain requested permission to unload the refugees. The Australian government, however, refused permission for the ship to enter Christmas Island terriotorial waters, citing the inadequacy of the island's facilities to cope with such numbers. Others knew the underlying reason, however, as the growing unrest in Australia over the number of immigrants and asylum seekers. If these people set foot on Australian soil, the argument went, they could legitimately claim asylum. In addition, there was to be a general election within months.

This then exploded into a diplomatic fracas, involving Australia, Indonesia, Norway, the UN and NGOs such as Amnesty International. The weight of international opinion was against the Australian government. Norway reported the country to the UN and the International Maritime Organisation for forgoing their obligations and Amnesty International criticised Australia, by accusing it of violating the UN Refugee Convention.

Eventually a solution was brokered which had the Australian government paying for the refugees' carriage to the Pacific island of Nauru – the world's smallest republic.

Rinnan was given the Nansen award for 2002 from the UNHCR for his efforts to follow international principles for rescuing people at sea, despite threats from the Australian government to imprison him and impound his ship.

Analysis

Where did Australia go wrong? Asylum seekers are one of the problems of our day and, excluding the difficult and complicated reasons as to why they exist, how should states deal with them? Democratically elected leaders must pay attention to their electorate or face the consequences. In addition, a neutral ship's captain who had rescued hundreds of people from certain death seemed to be vilified by the government. A more pragmatic approach, with swifter outcomes, should have been adopted. Accept some of the refugees (say, women and children) and then broker with Indonesia for the rest. In the end it was likely that all of them could have ended up in the same place but dealing with the problem efficiently would have kept the issue out of the media at a crucial pre-election time.

There are other crises in which a politician has no choice but to become involved. For example, when there is a major catastrophe, and particularly if there is a loss of life.

THE MADRID BOMBING

On Thursday March 11 2004, Madrid witnessed the most catastrophic terrorist incident in Europe since the crash of Pan Am flight 103 in 1988. The Spanish capital was hit by 10 bombs exploding on four trains in three stations during the early morning rush hour. The attack was coordinated and dramatic and had been designed to create chaos and take the lives of as many Spaniards as possible.

At 07.39 three bombs exploded in the third, fourth and sixth carriages of a train which had just pulled into the busy Atoche station in the centre of Madrid. Four further bombs exploded in another train just behind the first. Down the line at El Pozo station a train passing through the area was rocked by explosions in two of its carriages, and a minute later a fourth train was hit as it passed through Santa Eugenia station. It was later discovered that the bombs had been remotely detonated using mobile telephones.

The initial reports were hazy and the scale of the atrocity was unclear. Throughout the day, however, 24 news stations beamed the scenes of devastation into the homes of millions throughout the world and the horror of the situation became all too apparent. Reporters were quick to realise the importance of this event. With just under 200 people killed and thousands of others injured, this was an act of terrorism previously unparalleled in Europe.

However, this case study does not examine the incident itself nor the handling of it by the Spanish emergency services, but rather the reaction to the events of the Spanish government, led by Jose Maria Aznar.

Almost directly the reports of the bombings entered the global news arena, questions were asked as to who the perpetrators of this crime were. Because of the scale of the event and the dramatic death toll, people's minds turned to al-Qaeda and September 11. With war in Iraq dominating the news agenda and polarising the international community, was this the Islamic terrorists' first major 'successful' mission in Europe? Pundits pointed to the fact that Spain and the UK were the only European countries with substantial levels of troops in Iraq in support of US forces.

'No, not so', said the Spanish government. Aznar appeared on national television. Clearly grief-stricken by the tragedy of the event, he was quick to state who he believed was behind the attack. The Spanish prime minister argued that the evidence pointing towards the Basque separatist group ETA was incontrovertible.

At first this assumption appeared reasonable. ETA is the major terrorist group within Spain. Formed in 1959 whilst the country was under the dictatorship of Franco, the movement set about the task of securing an independent state for the Basque people. Since then the group has targeted Spanish politicians and more recently tourist hotspots like the Costa del Sol to make its case. Up until then, however, ETA had been involved in relatively small-scale terrorist incidents. This would have represented a dramatic shift in tactics.

Aznar has a personal history with ETA. He was once the subject of an assassination attempt by the group and, since being elected to government in 1996, has vowed to wipe out the organisation. This personal battle was later used by some to accuse the prime minister of prematurely concluding that ETA was behind the attacks.

The world's media and politicians appeared to take Aznar's comments at face value. News commentators and opinion writers in national papers all concluded that this represented a dramatic shift in tactics for the group but that nevertheless it was responsible. The Spaniards themselves also believed their government. Millions took to the streets of Madrid, Seville and Barcelona to protest against terrorism. Many banners simply read 'No to ETA'. In a moving scene, the people of the Basque city of Bilbao walked silently through the city centre, poignantly sending their own message to, supposedly, those who were fighting for their independence.

The international community was so convinced by the Spanish government's insistence that ETA was responsible that an emergency meeting of the UN Security Council was held officially to denounce the acts of ETA. George Bush, president of the USA, and Tony Blair, prime minister of the UK, both central figures in the campaign against terror, stood united with their Madrileño companion.

The Spanish government's mistake was to seem so certain of ETA's culpability. It also appeared to be withholding information about the attacks. How could the government be so certain; surely it must have been in possession of incriminating information? This and other questions began to make their way into the media. The government did not, however, respond directly.

Questions were raised again when evidence was found which linked the bombing to al-Qaeda. Tapes playing verses from the Koran were found in a car in the Madrid suburbs. News crews jumped on this. The Spanish government, however, remained unmoved.

At the time of the bombing, Spain was a country in the throes of an election campaign. The election was due to be held on the Sunday immediately following the bombings of Thursday. Against this backdrop, the media and the Spanish public began to question their leader's motives once the Islamic tapes were found.

The decision to go to war was hugely unpopular in Spain, with the vast majority of the public opposing the war. Aznar had been a popular prime minister and had enjoyed an extended period of office – a change from the largely socialist governments of the past. Spain was fast becoming a wealthy nation, a big player in the European club. Despite this success, Aznar's reputation had been significantly damaged by the decisions he made on Iraq. The last thing he wanted was an unavoidable reminder of this three days before the country went to the polls.

The Spanish public began to see things in light of this. The tone of the street protests changed. Banners appeared to attack Aznar as much as the terrorists. 'No to ETA' signs were noticeable by their absence. The government was slow to react. The crisis hit quickly as news changed throughout the day. By the evening of March 11 a letter was sent to the London-based Arabic newspaper *Al-Quds*. This letter was written on behalf of the Abu Hafs al-Masri Brigade, a terrorist group affiliated with al-Qaeda. The group claimed that it was responsible for the atrocity.

The Spanish government found itself forced into admitting that there were other possible culprits besides ETA. As ministers appeared on television, concessions were made – the government's line had changed – there was a possibility that it was someone else, but the government was still convinced that ETA was the number one suspect.

On March 13 five men were arrested following the discovery of a mobile phone inside a pack of explosives. On March 14 a video claiming responsibility for the attacks was found. The message was recorded by an al-Qaeda spokesman based in Europe and explained the reason for this act of revenge: '[for] collaboration with the criminal Bush and his allies'.

It was then that the Spanish government was backed into a corner. All the evidence now pointed towards al-Qaeda, not ETA. March 14 was the day of the election and by now the Spanish public had grown increasingly sceptical of their prime minister's assertions. Until the last minute the ruling Popular Party was on course to win the election, but with a reduced majority. As evidence emerged of the al-Qaeda link, the Spanish public reacted angrily. Voters turned up to the polling booths hurling abuse at the Popular Party workers, shouting 'manipulator' at Aznar as he cast his vote.

The election results came in early in the morning of March 15. The Socialist Workers' Party (not to be confused with the far left party of the UK) had won through, with 43 per cent of the vote and 164 seats in the Chamber of Deputies. The Popular Party (led by Rajoy after Aznar stood down) received only 37 per cent of the vote and won only 148 of the seats. This represented a dramatic turnaround in voting intentions.

Often when a nation is hit by a tragedy, the public rallies behind the current administration. War is a great unifier. However, the circumstances in Madrid were quite different.

The Popular Party managed not only to lose any of the goodwill it may have gained as a result of a united and newly patriotic country, but also contrived to lose heavily an election it was on course to win handsomely.

Categorising politicians

In most modern democracies, there are three broad levels of political activity:

- *Government.* In many democracies there are two houses – an upper house and a lower house, the Senate and Congress in the USA being an obvious example, and the House of Lords and House of Commons in the UK. In general, one of these has an executive role, and this is the more important one in a crisis.
- *Regional politics.* Countries with a federal structure will have a federal government, as is the case in Germany and the US. These often subsume many of the responsibilities and authorities of a national government.
- *Local government.* This is often subsegmented and local councils or communes are often the lowest tier in the tax-gathering hierarchy. In the UK, for example, local government is divided into county, district or borough level (often based around one city) and parish level which is around a small community.

In a crisis, all these levels of government must be briefed and mechanisms for contact must be put in place. No matter what their level of power or authority, politicians need to know what is happening in their communities, whether community is the whole country or one tiny village. Politicians do not like getting information directly from the media, because this information is often tainted as it has been passed to the media from yet another source. Politicians like to be *briefed*. In other words, they need to know the information before they are approached by someone else. They see this as a key part of their role as community leaders.

If they are blind-sided, they have a number of options, all of them bad for the company which is in crisis:

1. *Take the journalist's information as gospel.* This, as noted above, is dangerous. In a crisis, truth is an early casualty and comments based on untrue or distorted facts can be misleading. Unfortunately for the politician, U-turns are difficult manoeuvres to undertake and they are often stuck with the first comment. Certainly, it will come back to haunt them if they decide to change their mind.

For example, following a major disaster, say an explosion at a chemical plant, a politician, having been told that up to 50 people may have died, may say to the local media: 'This is an absolute disaster for my community and I will not rest until those who are responsible are brought to justice.' If it later transpires that there was a small explosion, causing only minor damage and no injuries, the politician is still stuck with the quote. He now looks doubly foolish as he has grossly overreacted to what was a non-incident. In the eyes of his community, he appears not to be in touch and to be isolated from those who pass out information, in other words, those in power. In essence, he looks ineffectual.

2. *Speculate.* This is equally dangerous. News-hungry journalists – anxious for a quote in order to round off their story – will often tend to ask leading questions. For example:

> Councillor Johnson, if it were the case that 50 people had died, how would you react to this?'

Unfortunately, the reaction is exactly that of above and has precisely the same effect. It is difficult for the politician to unhook himself at a later date.

3. *Try to get information from the company.* This is a responsible course of action, but if the politician has not had dealings with the company in the past, he will be scrabbling around for telephone numbers, email addresses and even names of those with whom he should be in contact. In a crisis, the key people will already be tied up in managing the crisis and so the politician is frustrated in his or her efforts to get any information from the company.

4. *Seek information from other sources.* In the absence of information from the company, the politician may go to other sources – often those which are not friendly towards the corporation. So if an activist group, for example, has commented on the activities of the corporation, the politician may remember this and go to it for his information. For obvious reasons, this is also dangerous.

5. *Information may come to the politician.* The enemies of a corporation – and few are the companies which do not have some – will be quick to see the vulnerability of the organisation in a crisis. If the activists are quick, they start issuing press releases, making calls and updating the website. As these groups are often quick off the mark, they may approach the key politicians and offer them briefings on their side of the story. With a vacuum of information, the politician may reach for this and take it as the truth.

In summary, a politician without information will react exactly as the columnist C Northcote Parkinson predicted in his quote:

> The vacuum created by failure to communicate will quickly be filled by rumour, misrepresentation, drivel and poison.

A politician without any other information will quickly begin to feed on this and the damage may be irreparable, both during the crisis and in the future.

The proactive approach

From the above, it is obvious that if a company or corporation does not put across its side of the story, the vacuum caused by a failure to communicate is soon filled with rumour, misrepresentation, drivel and poison.

However, there is little time for scrabbling around to put together a communication programme in the middle of a crisis. A crisis is like a major forest fire – it consumes all resources available to it and continues to demand more. There is no time to plan in a crisis. Preparation, therefore, must include all of the following:

1. A thorough and understandable research document, the 'diagnostic' of who are the key players and who might be affected should the company have a crisis. A diagnostic is effectively a review of key stakeholders and issues that may affect or play a part with the company (described in Chapter 11).
2. A 'stakeholder segmentation' exercise to decide who is key to the company's survival, its wellbeing, and who will attack it (also described in Chapter 11).
3. It is essential to gather together details of how these people may be contacted. It is a rare chancellor or prime minister, however, who hands out their own home numbers on the Internet. So their organisations must be contacted well in advance to ensure that there is a legitimate route by which to reach key people. For example, many government departments are willing to have their civil servants be the first point of contact who can then sift the information and pass it on as necessary. There is a risk here that the information may not be passed on in time, but it is better to have this conduit in place rather than have nothing. It is also important that this interface is at the highest possible level.

It takes time to build these contacts and to win their trust in order to ensure that the recipients see the legitimacy of the company's need to be in a position to communicate with it in a crisis. However, if this is 'sold' carefully, with understanding, then most government departments and politicians will react favourably.

When sensitive information, mobile phone numbers, private emails, and so on, is received, it is absolutely essential that it remains confidential and is only shared among those in the crisis management team.

The protocol of dealing with politicians

As noted earlier, politicians hate to be blind-sided and do not like to get their information second-hand. They believe that they have been elected by their communities and their constituents to *represent* them. This is not the role of the media. Too often, organisations are most keen to brief the media, leaving politicians and other key stakeholders behind.

Although the media have huge power in influencing what people think about, it is worth remembering that their power is not in changing politicians' minds, it is in setting the agenda. As stated earlier, the media may not be spectacularly successful at telling people *what to think* – after all, if you do not agree with what a paper says, you stop buying it – but it is spectacularly successful in telling readers *what to think about*. Politicians are not immune.

Therefore, whilst the media have influence, they cannot, by themselves, put a company out of business. Politicians – through their regulatory powers – certainly can. One should never forget this.

CALIFORNIA POWER CUTS

To many, California is represented as the holy grail of the hi-tech world. This rich state has an iconic quality, heralded as the apotheosis of the American dream, with its sun-kissed, wealthy, happy beautiful people. Yet in 2001, it was subjected to the first mandatory power cut since World War II.

The problems arose after the unsuccessful liberalisation of the energy industry in 1996. Companies such as Southern California Edison and Pacific Gas & Electric were the initial beneficiaries of this liberalisation as they were handed what they thought would be lucrative contracts. However, the companies ran into financial trouble and to balance the books decided to close a number of their power stations and reduce investment. This proved unsustainable as California's economy continued to boom. Essentially, California was running out of energy as more and more users placed a drain on the system.

Energy had to be shipped in from other locations to avoid power cuts. This meant that the cost of energy provision rose sharply. Deregulation was meant to result in supposed lower costs for the consumer, but in reality it had led to price hikes as the companies pushed costs on to the consumer. Californians reacted against this. They took their protests to the federal government and sought political assistance to stop the companies overcharging. In August 2000, the US administration decided to take action and capped charges.

The effect of this price capping acted as a catalyst for the energy crisis. Energy providers argued that because they were unable to pass on the increased costs of energy provision to the consumer, they were now facing near bankruptcy.

Further bad news came when in January 2001 storms hit California. To meet demand, the power companies were forced to buy electricity at prices 10 times higher than the previous year.

Analysis

The companies failed to avoid a crisis because of a number of decisions. Firstly they had not planned for worst-case scenarios. The business plan had clearly not anticipated the growth of the economy, nor had it correctly costed the price of importing electricity. Of course with the arrival of storms, Murphy's Law had really taken hold. The companies then took the ill-advised step of coming into conflict with their customers and, by implication, the politicians who represented them. By refusing to bend to their demands and not appearing to offer the public anything to hold on to, the electricity companies appeared arrogant and at odds with the people they were trying to win over.

The regulators

Today most modern corporations are, in effect, broadly self-regulating. Even in the vital area of tax collection, most countries have high levels of self-assessment. In addition, companies have their own internal audit teams which monitor financial performance, look out for fraud and seek to ensure the company gets best value. Overall, good self-regulation makes good sense and links into good corporate responsibility.

In most modern democracies, the elected representatives are supported by a civil service or unelected officials. Among these are the regulators. Although independent of the elected representatives, they work closely with them and their policies are often set by the government of the day. They cover areas such as finance, for example the Financial Services Authority in the UK and the environment, for example the USA's Environmental Protection Agency, as well as the style and type of houses which can be constructed, through building regulations and planning permits.

Regulators can also be spread across all tiers of government – from the national level right down to the local council or community parish council.

However, they are often treated like internal auditors: performing an important function, but at the same time often seen by operating divisions as little more than a nuisance. Certainly they have to slow – and sometimes stop – the flow of work so that they can go about their business. This can generate resentment.

Similarly, government regulators are seen in the same light. For an organisation that is prone to crisis, this is a dangerous position to adopt. When a crisis strikes, there is little doubt that the regulator will have to be involved, almost from the beginning. Therefore, it is prudent and good business practice to ensure that they follow these rules:

- *Make sure they are aware of your crisis management procedures.* If the regulators are knowledgeable about your procedures and how you are going to react, it gives them a strong comfort factor. At worst, they know that you are planning for emergencies and that fact, in itself, is the sign of a responsible organisation. The point at which the regulator becomes involved in the crisis should also be delineated and agreed.

- *Have good contacts.* As part of the crisis management procedures, it is essential that people within the company know which *named individuals* within the regulatory body are to be contacted and at what point. Rather like a rugby lineout, each person in the organisation should have a specific regulatory body to deal with. Obviously, they will have telephone numbers, mobile telephone numbers, emails and so on.

- *Involve them in your testing procedures.* At the annual or biannual test, it is good to have the regulator play his or her own role. This way the organisation will get an insight into the mindset of the regulators, what they are looking for and how they may react. Relationships are strengthened and tensions are reduced.

REGULATORS UNDER THE MICROSCOPE

In the UK each August thousands of 18-year-olds await the results of examinations which could determine the course of their adult life in the UK. A-level results day is for some a joyous occasion which rewards two years of hard work with a place at their chosen university. For others, the day is less of a cause for celebration as disappointed students who have failed to get their required grades decide what to do next.

In 2002, however, the situation was quite different from normal as students were left wondering whether their results were worth the paper they were written on.

The scandal centred on the accusation that A-level papers had been deliberately marked down, because of political pressure to keep the number of people attaining the top marks under control. Many teenagers' dreams were shattered as they found that their actual grades bore no relation to their predicted grades and consequently university places which they thought were theirs no longer were.

The crisis hit the public domain when head teachers across the country questioned the results, and ultimately demanded an inquiry. The crisis threatened to rock the education system to its foundations. The national papers lamented the fall in standards and seemed to write off a whole generation of school leavers. Industrialists expressed concern that employers would no longer place trust in the A-level system.

The efforts to bring the crisis under control were first made by the decision to hold an inquiry into the scandal by someone who was – in effect – an independent regulator, so meeting the demands of head teachers.

The Tomlinson Report was published on September 27 and sought to answer all the questions posed by the public in the weeks following results day. The report concluded that pressure had been brought to bear on examination boards to keep the results down, so that they would be in line with those achieved the following year.

The report recommended that some A-level papers should be re-marked. This gave some students some cheer, but equally importantly a recognition of their situation. The government also announced that universities would honour offers made to students whose grades may be marked up. A caveat was added to this: universities which had already filled their spaces would have to ask students to defer for a year if they still wished to take up their place.

Analysis
The report provided a focal point for the anger and anxiety of those involved. The report, although it could not serve as complete closure, would act as a sign of action being taken – as a mark in the sand. The independent regulator had a key role in taking pressure off the government. In effect, the regulator acted as a third party advocate.

The questions about the education system still remain, and efforts are being made to change the way in which the nation's young adults are tested. However, this crisis was contained by the setting up of an independent inquiry – yet another quasi-regulator – which conveniently led to minimal heads rolling, but produced the results most had wanted.

Regulators and the media

As soon as a crisis becomes public, it is likely that the regulator will be immediately contacted for a comment by the media. They will also be asked for assurance or otherwise by politicians. Generally, they will also come under fierce pressure from activist groups who will immediately condemn the organisation in crisis, particularly if relationships with the activist groups have been acrimonious. They will also put pressure on the regulatory agencies to come out against the company in crisis.

If the regulator does not have the comfort of knowing that the organisation is handling the crisis well, then he or she may well bow to that pressure.

It is essential, therefore, at an early stage, to inform regulators that there may be a problem. To adapt the old adage from Northern Irish politics (vote early, vote often), companies in crisis should: 'Contact early, contact often.' Organisations can be reticent and so there are feelings in some organisations that they do not want to be seen 'crying wolf' all the time and wasting energies. Again, this is a dangerous attitude. Regulators hate to be blind-sided.

Regulators as third party advocates

Regulators not only have to be independent, they have to be seen to be independent. Often this means that their public position is much harder than their private stance. This is important and is, paradoxically, useful.

If the regulator is involved in a crisis from the beginning – and is seen to be involved – he/she is also part of the problem and, potentially, the solution. It can be reassuring for politicians, the media and the public to see that the regulator has been involved. Although their comments may be critical and harsh at times, it is better to have them inside rather than outside.

However, regulators, who are publicly funded for the most part, can be slow to involve themselves in a public stance on the crisis. They may at some stage have to stand in judgement on the crisis and comments made now can come back to haunt them.

However, if the crisis-stricken organisation can openly say that it has been in dialogue with its regulators from an early stage, then it has shown openness and honesty, which is extremely reassuring.

Conclusion

Politicians will tend to avoid becoming embroiled in a crisis, but there are times when they must get involved. A proactive approach – realising that they are the ultimate regulators – is the best approach.

So the first steps must be to contact the key politicians and their bureaucracies very early on in the crisis. Without pestering those in power or who regulate power, it is important that they are fully briefed and even if the crisis fizzles out, they will appreciate being alerted well in advance.

CHAPTER 8

The Activists: Making Crises Happen

Beginning with the environmental groups in the 1960s, today activist groups surround almost every industry and sector. The environmental movement is now a huge industry, with turnovers measured in billions of dollars. Although they try to portray themselves as altruistic amateurs, nothing could be further from the truth. These are finely honed, well-financed and highly efficient publicity machines. Just ask Shell, Exxon, Monsanto, Nestlé or almost any multinational.

Manufacturing a crisis

A crisis is a clarion call to the NGOs. When they are on television as pundits and experts, lobbying government around the issues that caused the crisis, they are suddenly seen to be independent experts.

NESTLÉ v OXFAM

From its involvement in milk powder as a substitute for breast milk, Nestlé has been a target for left-wing activist groups. The logic of having a substitute for those mothers who could not produce enough milk – a not uncommon occurrence in famine-stricken Africa – was not a consideration for activists. Nor was the fact that the company was no longer involved in this business. When mud is thrown, it sticks.

The company is intrinsically linked with stories of third world exploitation. In many ways, this is most unfair. For example, in June 2002 – the year of the Ethiopian crisis – Nestlé gave €2 million to a Red Cross initiative aimed at fighting HIV/AIDS in Africa, prompting the Red Cross to call for more corporate support for health programmes in Africa. Corporate social responsibility indeed. In fact, the Red Cross praised Nestlé by saying that more companies should give in this manner.

On December 18, 2002 — and the timing close to Christmas is crucial — the third world charity Oxfam disclosed that Nestlé was demanding millions of dollars in compensation from famine-stricken Ethiopia. At the time, the country was experiencing an extreme drought that put over 11 million people at risk of starvation. Simultaneously, the price of coffee beans, one of Ethiopia's main export earners, had fallen, exacerbating the country's crisis. Nestlé is the world's largest coffee company.

Nestlé claimed that it was owed $6 million as compensation for a business owned by a German company — since taken over by Nestlé — that was seized by Ethiopia's military dictatorship in 1975. Oxfam was quick to point out in its press briefing materials that Nestlé turned a profit of Swfr 6.68 billion ($3.92 billion) in 2001 and its annual sales amounted to about Swfr 85 billion. During the first half of 2002, the group's net profit grew 79 per cent to Swfr 5.65 billion compared to the same period a year earlier.

For its part, the Ethiopian government had also offered Nestlé a settlement of around $1.6 million which the company had refused to accept. This issue centres around exchange rates; Nestlé worked at 1975 exchange rates, Ethiopia offered it at the current exchange rate. It was offering what it thought was a fair price. Oxfam then launched its campaign against the coffee giant's actions, attacking it both for the timing and the principle of its demands.

But getting people to boycott Nestlé coffee products would also damage the people of Ethiopia, who produced the beans. So Oxfam was clever in its approach. 'Boycotting Nestlé products won't help the poor farmers who sell to the company,' said Justin Forsyth, head of policy at Oxfam. 'What people should do if they want to help is to write or email Nestlé and ask it to drop the claim.'

Almost immediately, 8500 people had emailed the company to complain about its treatment of the Ethiopian government, the fastest response Oxfam ever had to a campaign. In all some 40,000 wrote to Nestlé to protest. A crisis had indeed been manufactured.

Nestlé was quick to react — as fast as a multinational can be when it is trying to find out what is happening in a developing country with poor communications. By Tuesday, December 23 — five days later — Peter Brabeck, the company's chief executive, made an announcement admitting that he had been taken by surprise by a demonstration outside Nestlé's British offices. This forced the company — in the period just before Christmas — to promptly scramble to find 'an external Ethiopian lawyer engaged by a small German subsidiary of Nestlé Germany who is handling the sporadic negotiations'.

Mr Brabeck said that as the Ethiopian government has already offered $1.6 million, it would immediately make this sum available for famine relief in Ethiopia.

It also reacted well by using third party advocates — even though the Red Cross proved be a slightly hesitant bride. Mr Brabeck said Nestlé had asked the International Federation of the Red Cross and Red Crescent societies on 'how best to direct' additional funds.

The Red Cross confirmed that it had just been contacted by the Swiss multinational but that it was still in internal negotiations and that any response would be premature. The Red Cross has more in common with Oxfam than it has with Nestlé, despite the $2 million donation for HIV/AIDS work earlier in the year.

That should have been the end of the matter. Europe was heading into Christmas and the festivities would soon banish all thoughts of Ethiopia. But this crisis – as most of them do – carried on. Nestlé had a sting in the tail. Mr Brabeck also announced: 'We will do the same with any additional sums resulting from a final settlement,' indicating that Nestlé had not given up further compensation.

Nestlé continued to insist that it would be good for Ethiopia to pay the rest of the money owed to it. 'It is in the Ethiopian government's interest to reach a deal as a way to ensure continued flows of foreign direct investment in the country,' said a company spokesman. 'We are flexible about the timing and the amount but we are not flexible about the principle.'

Naturally, this gave a story another fillip. Oxfam was back. The aid agency dismissed Nestlé's claim that Ethiopia will find it hard to attract foreign investors unless it pays the compensation bill. Its spokesperson said: 'This is absurd and unfair. This is not about legal rights but what is morally right. When 11 million people face famine, exceptions should be made. I hope that Nestlé reconsiders and realises they don't need the money as much as Ethiopia. I hope they drop the issue altogether.'

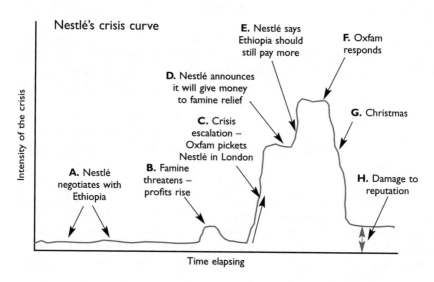

Analysis

Oxfam chose the days before Christmas, in essence, ensuring that Murphy's Law and its corollaries were in place from the start. Like it or not, large organisations allow their people to take holidays near Christmas and guards are down.

Newspaper journalists were quick to see the appeal of the story. Here was the west – in a bout of rampant consumerism – and a giant corporation which was trying to get money from a famine-stricken country. Journalists also drew on the Band Aid song 'Do they know it's Christmas?' as part of their headline writing.

Returning to the crisis diagram, it can be seen that a crisis will rumble along the bottom of the curve for a long period of time before it actually erupts. This is true of almost all the crises which are featured in this book. There was the whole concept of negotiating with a developing country for what is a paltry sum while profits were rising. Again – in hindsight – it is easy to see this. It is not as simple in the day-to-day running of a business; especially as Nestlé saw what it was doing as the right solution.

However, there is a key point (C) when a crisis could have been curtailed. This was immediately as Oxfam went public with its press release. Whilst it is easy with hindsight to indicate what should have been done, it is obvious that Nestlé, at this stage, should have decided, as it eventually had to do, to wipe out the debt. A difficult task. Communications with Ethiopia in the pre-Christmas period would not have been easy, communications with developing countries never are.

Once a crisis goes into trajectory (point C), it is almost impossible to pull it back. As seen earlier, the media will become interested and as the media watches the media, the crisis will escalate further and further. Rather like an arrow unleashed from a bow, it is impossible to pull it back and retrieve the arrow after it has left. This is exactly the case with a crisis.

Nestlé, which has its critics, is a forward-thinking, modern company which most independent commentators would agree tries to do its best by its customers, suppliers and its stakeholders. However, even with its huge resources, it was caught rudely unawares when a pressure group decided to attack it.

The damage done from the breast milk substitute days has stuck and this is something from which the company will take a very long time (decades) to recover. It must accept this. Any business plan will have to factor this in and any crisis management strategy must be aware of this situation. The sheer size of the company has meant that it has been able to withstand the negative publicity and the boycotting of its products. However, these crises are damaging to the brand and the company must ensure they do not happen again. In a huge organisation, operating in almost every country in the world, with differing cultures, this is indeed a tall order.

For Oxfam, this was a coup. It had generated huge publicity – not just in the UK – but throughout the world.

The NGOs as marketeers

As the activists grew in power and maturity, they realised that they should have a more influential role with government. In a classic rebranding exercise, they emerged in the late 1980s as non-governmental organisations (NGOs). The name has stuck and although it is meaningless – any organisation which is not part of the government is a non-governmental organisation – it is used in this book, given its huge currency.

As in any economic segment, there is competition between the various environmental corporations. So, if you ask Friends of the Earth which organisation poses the greatest threat to it, it should answer Greenpeace. It seeks the same members and so competes for funds.

The NGOs, however, now know that their marketplace is big enough for there to be a piece of the action for everyone. So there has – either consciously or unconsciously – been a market segmentation exercise. So Greenpeace does whales, Oxfam concentrates on developing states issues and the Worldwide Fund for Nature does furry animals.

Despite the competition, the NGOs are far better than mainstream corporations at forming strategic alliances. They are willing to set aside their differences and work together. Of course, companies have trade associations to represent them, but these are never as effective as direct cooperation on the ground.

However, whilst many people support the aims of these organisations, not all are members, so the NGOs have ongoing marketing campaigns through the usual methods used by mainstream corporations: direct mail, press relations campaigns, advertising and the like. These are expensive to mount, but there are more and more of them, so the NGOs, whilst decrying the modern communications industry, have little hesitation in using its methods and becoming reference standards in the industry. These groups try to play down their PR activities, which they prefer to call campaigning and they are among the most effective publicists in the world.

NGOs and democracy

Unlike governments, these organisations are not elected by anyone. For example, green groups – as reasonably reflected by the Green Party – poll particularly badly in democratic elections, with the possible exception of Germany. Here they became part of Schroeder's power-sharing government in 1998 and control a number of regional assemblies. The Green Party is also represented in the French cabinet. However, in most countries, the green vote is well below 5 per cent.

It is not suggested for a moment that minorities – no matter how insignificant – do not have a right to be heard. They do. But only within the framework of a democratic society and its laws. The acts of Greenpeace on the uprooting of trials of GM plants in the UK were outside the law.

This was justified by Greenpeace in an article in *The Times,* July 31, 1999:

I am clear that what we did was not illegal. We were justified in removing this pollution…The paradox is that Greenpeace is only ever accused of being undemocratic when we represent the views of millions of people in a way which can't be ignored.

Nor should there be any further curtailment on the right to protest – always enshrined in a modern democracy. The only caveat is that protest should be within the law, and, in particular, it should not cause wilful damage to private property – as was the case with the GM crops protest.

Politicians and NGOs

Politicians, outside the green parties, are also quick to associate themselves with environmental causes and a great many are members of Friends of the Earth, Greenpeace and so on. In particular, the environment is a motherhood cause and is fairly safe from attack.

Members of national parties in many countries are active members of NGOs. This in part explains why the Green Party never does particularly well. Someone else has stolen its clothes.

Broadly, politicians would like to be on the side of the NGOs, particularly if they are fighting a faceless multinational. David will always get more support than Goliath.

The media and NGOs

There is a strong symbiotic relationship between NGOs and the media. At the start, NGOs are often seen to represent the smaller organisation or individual. This sort of campaigning is very much in tune with the journalist's own crusades to expose truth, fight corruption and generally be guardians of the common good.

In addition, the media (see Chapter 7) also has a strong role to entertain and, of course, NGOs can often provide an entertaining or horrific story. For example, Nestlé demanding money from the Ethiopian government, violence (*Brent Spar*) and horror (Frankenstein foods). Therefore the media is happy to be fed stories by green groups.

The media is also about speculation – it is the substance of most political stories. Therefore when the NGOs speculate in a crisis, the media is more than happy to take this speculation as fact. The NGOs and the media can both work on the Law of the Absolute. So to the question, 'Can you promise that this incident will not cause any damage now or in the future?', the answer has to be 'I don't know' or 'no'.

Dealing with NGOs

In dealing with NGOs, often it is helpful to use a moderator who is neutral. Universities can provide a neutral forum and a neutral moderator in the form of a senior professor or lecturer. The debate then can move to some of the scientific issues surrounding the organisation's plans and the NGO's objections to them. Also by meeting on neutral ground, it gives added credibility to the discussions, as there is no hint that the organisation is trying to brainwash, persuade or manipulate the NGO.

An NGO is diametrically opposed to the aims and ambitions of the organisation with which it is dealing. For example, Greenpeace is totally opposed to nuclear power and GM foods. Therefore, is there any point in a dialogue? The answer is yes for a number of reasons.

First, good corporate social responsibility dictates that an organisation should deal with all its stakeholders – even those totally opposed to it. Even if no progress can be made in dialogue, it is good to be seen having that dialogue. So for example, the nuclear industry will regularly sit down with Greenpeace. This gives an advantage to the industry, in that it can say to government: 'We are good corporate citizens in that we talk to all our stakeholders, not just those who support us.' For Greenpeace, there is also a benefit. It can be seen to be a responsible NGO – rather than just an activist group – and it too gets further credibility with the government. For both sides, the name of the game is to keep face and increase their profile.

So it is important to engage in a dialogue at an early stage with NGOs. As part of the stakeholder segmentation exercise (see Chapter 11), these groups will have been identified. They should then be approached.

In general, the approach should be informal and early meetings should have little or no agenda. An agenda will evolve over time. Certainly, the objective of the NGO may be, say, to shut a plant or stop a process, but there are a number of issues around the main objective with which the organisation can deal with the NGO. For example, there can be an agreement on information sharing. One has to be careful here, of course, to ensure that others – particularly the government and regulators – are also getting the same information so that they are not blind-sided by the NGO, who may seek to take immediate advantage.

Who should undertake this work?

This is definitely not a job for the chief executive or indeed the most senior people in the company. However, it needs to be seen to be taken seriously – as it is a serious matter – and the task should be delegated to a senior manager – ideally, someone who has a deep knowledge of the issues which are involved. The corporate communications department also has a role here in ensuring that the company's line is maintained and that key messages are fine-tuned before these meetings.

Conclusion

NGOs can be powerful in generating a crisis, as Nestlé found out in Ethiopia. They are also magnetically drawn to a crisis as it provides an excellent marketing opportunity. As part of any crisis management procedure, dealing with NGOs is an important part of the process and should be considered carefully.

The objective here is not to win round NGOs but to ensure that they are aware of the organisation's position. Certainly during a crisis, they may still choose to attack the company, but they have to do it with the full knowledge that they know the real facts, even if they choose to ignore them. It also leaves the organisation in a much stronger position, in that it can say it has been in dialogue with all its stakeholders including those who vehemently oppose it. This gives added credibility during a crisis.

CHAPTER 9

Other Stakeholders: Dealing with the Public, Customers and Suppliers

As soon as a crisis breaks in the media, it will immediately attract public attention. For most people, the crisis will generate idle curiosity and little else. They will take the information given to them by the media, make their judgements on it and move on. However, a small minority – for whatever reason – will take a more direct interest. This small minority can sometimes be just hundreds or, at other times, thousands of people. For example, if a bank has a problem with hackers getting into its systems, potentially almost all the bank's customers are affected. This can be millions of people and thousands of these will be concerned that the details of their accounts have been made public. These people can vary from the naturally paranoid to errant fathers who have not been paying proper maintenance for their children and are keeping their financial details secret from their former spouses.

SPAM EMAILS

In November 2003, the usual flood of spam emails entering people's inboxes had a criminal flavour. A spate of emails from spammers attempted to fool people into entering their private security data for online banking. Potential victims are encouraged to verify their account information on fraudulent sites which posed as the real thing.

This information would then be collected by the spammers and used to defraud customers of their money. These fraudulent emails were sent to numerous people using spamming software in the hope of reeling in a few victims, and accounted for almost one in ten spam messages at their peak.

Halifax Bank, one of the institutions mentioned in the emails, took almost immediate action. Well aware that there is already huge suspicion about the Internet and security, it took the major step of taking its ebanking site offline in response to the widespread circulation of these fraudulent emails targeting its customers.

In a statement emailed to customers, Halifax said: 'In the interests of the security of our customers we have temporarily closed the online service in order that we can communicate the issue to online customers and to make improvements in the service to further safeguard online accounts. Please note that we would never send you emails that ask for confidential or personal security information.'

A spokesman for the bank later commented: 'We felt it was better to bring the site down and make changes and then bring everything back up together. We want to tackle the problem in its totality.'

Analysis

Although this move did inconvenience some customers, it proved that the bank was putting the concerns of its customers first and foremost. No doubt the move did create extra work for the bank in taking more queries by telephone or at branches, but it was seen to be doing the right thing. It also engaged the consumer by calling on its ebank customers to be alert, and making sure that this event did not turn into a crisis of confidence.

An organisation can expect to receive hundreds of telephone calls in a short period of time after a crisis breaks. It must be prepared for this.

Dealing with the public in a crisis

Unlike the media and politicians, most members of the public only want the top line facts. For instance, if, during a storm, the power lines are knocked down and electricity is cut off, the question everyone asks is: 'When will the power come back on?'

In the banking crisis mentioned above, the question is: 'Have my details been put in jeopardy?' If, for example, only a tiny number of customers' details were affected, then it is easy to reassure all the rest. A simple statement which says: 'We have contacted all those customers who have been affected. If you have not been contacted, it means that the confidentiality of your account has not been breached' will satisfy the vast majority of people.

WILDCAT STRIKES

In late October 2003, British Royal Mail staff began small-scale strike action. Initially the strike broke out in small, localised pockets in London. By the second week, the strikes had spread to Chelmsford, Colchester, Coventry, Maidstone, Milton Keynes, Oxford,

Portsmouth, Slough, Southend and Swindon. In reality though, much of the country was affected, as one-fifth of the country's mail passes through London.

As the crisis deepened and millions of letters were stuck, the Royal Mail took the dramatic step of sealing up post boxes and urging people not to send any post at all. Effectively this is the Royal Mail's nuclear option – to stop the service it is supposed to provide. At the time, many predicted that this strike could have permanently reduced the Royal Mail's share of the market.

After the crisis was over, the company went about trying to restore its image and its place in the British psyche. As a goodwill gesture, the Royal Mail donated £1 million to London's bid for the 2012 Olympic Games to apologise for the effects of the strike. Chief Executive Adam Crozier explained: 'This is a donation that benefits the UK. We let our customers down and this is a straightforward way to say sorry.'

Analysis

This is a classic case of how things got worse before they got better. First, the strike spread from isolated cases to widespread action and, second, the action taken by the Royal Mail effectively suspended the service it provides. However, by taking this drastic action, things began to get under control. The media offensive from the company afterwards is recognition from senior management that it had lost ground in the marketplace. The worst was over, but efforts to rebuild the public's trust must be continued to avoid another crisis occurring.

As always, preparation is key.

The media as a TPA in dealing with the public

As most members of the public will find out about a crisis from the media, the media has a powerful role in turning messages from the organisation. It is also deemed to be independent and messages from the media are much more believed than those from the organisation. In effect, the media can act as a third party advocate.

Therefore it is essential that media are briefed early and given correct information. It is also essential – as we saw in Chapter 6 on the media – that third party advocates from other organisations, for instance the regulators, feature in the media.

AIR FRANCE CONCORDE

To many, Concorde was the ultimate flying machine, graceful and elegant yet powerful and expeditious. It was symbolic of an era; iconic in its association with rich, famous and glamorous people; and unrivalled in its appeal.

On July 25, 2000 these dreams came to a tragic end. Flight AF4590, an Air France Concorde en route to New York from Charles de Gaulle airport, crashed shortly after taking off. The aircraft crashed in flames into the Hotelissimo hotel in Gonesse, just two minutes north of Paris.

The full horror was captured on the hand-held video camera of an eye witness. The tragic frailty of the swanlike plane falling to earth seemed all the more poignant replayed through the amateur camerawork of a passerby. The images were beamed around the world.

The severity of the situation was immediately recognised. Not only had 113 people lost their lives, but the entire future of Concorde lay in the balance. How would the public react to the shocking images? Would confidence ever be restored in the aeroplane? Would people think that this signalled the end for an aircraft already over 25 years old?

The company acted quickly and decisively to manage the crisis. The first thing it did was to realise the importance of key stakeholders to the success of Concorde. Concorde is clearly not a product for everyone; it is out of most people's price range. For the wealthy, however, Concorde is seen as perhaps the only way to travel. There is a feeling of an elite club of flyers who use the airline. It was recognised that Concorde must appeal to these customers, to reassure them that they would be able to fly on the aircraft with absolute security in the future. The chief executive then took the move of contacting customers. The best customers, that is, the customers who flew most regularly, were contacted personally by the chief executive whilst thousands of others were contacted by a personally signed letter. This showed that the company cared and that it valued its customers. It also helped maintain that feeling of belonging to a club, encouraging customers to associate themselves with the fate of the aircraft, taking a stakehold in its future.

Crucially, the company continued this programme of contact. The customers were kept up to date with developments over the weeks and months following the crash, with newsletters and seminars.

Analysis

Eventually, Concorde flew again and it seemed to those involved that they had got their extraordinary product back. The crisis was managed because of visible and immediate leadership and the company's willingness to talk openly and candidly about the tragedy and the efforts to rectify the problems with the ageing aircraft. The crisis eventually saw the plane withdrawn from service throughout the world, but the reputation of Air France was enhanced.

Nowadays, we are dealing with a public which is far more aware. It is essential to remember this.

SECTION C

Design, Testing and Implementation

CHAPTER 10

Overview of the Process

Putting a crisis management plan into action does not have to be a long and arduous process; however, it does have to be approached methodically. The process needs to start with a discussion of what one would like to see as an outcome, what are the key aims of installing a crisis management procedure and how can these be put into place?

Throughout the process, these aims need to be kept in mind. What are we doing this for? How will this help the company? These will help to keep the process from becoming bureaucratic and overweight. It is essential that the development of crisis management procedures is given time. This time, however, must be channelled in the right direction and enthusiasm and motivation maintained.

There are essentially three important elements to any crisis management plan:

1. Most important, the *people* that make up the crisis management team. This group of individuals has to be carefully picked to reflect not just skills but personalities to ensure they can work together as a team and also work well under pressure. These people will underpin the whole process and time needs to be taken in their selection.
2. The *processes*, how the team will work, what guidelines and parameters the team will be set and what resources will be available to them. This is all covered within the crisis management handbook – the processes 'bible'. Testing and refining the procedures is extremely important to help keep the crisis management process organic and flexible – as every good crisis management plan should be.
3. *Environment*, where the team will work, what resources are required to keep the team running and how best to ensure that the environment is the best place to actually work. Should a dedicated room be consid-

ered? Are there enough telephone lines, fax machines and computers which will be used exclusively by the team?

It is these three elements that underpin any crisis management procedure. Before anyone embarks on such uncharted territory, however, they must know what they are working with. Scoping out the needs of the company and what the company already has in place is the springboard for crisis management procedures. It is important that this pool of knowledge – be it formal or informal – is fed into the emerging procedure. This is crucial both in building a cohesive and understandable strategy, but also in bringing along the rest of the company.

This assessment should look at:

- How the company has coped previously in a crisis situation
- What procedures are already in place
- Whether the existing procedures work well
- Whether they have been tested before, and what were the results
- Whether there are any employees who can add value to the process within the company.

By looking carefully at what is already there, ideas begin to emerge on how to evolve them – be they bulky and bureaucratic pieces of documentation that have yet to be read or flexible thought processes. In some respects, it is better to have none at all rather than have overenthusiastic and restrictive guidelines, procedures, rules and regulations. After all, one cannot be bound or held back by what is not there. This is also a potentially dangerous situation, however, and can lead to the headless chicken syndrome.

Building on this background, it is important to have buy-in to any processes which are introduced. Therefore this has to be backed by everyone, from top management to those on the ground. It should not be seen as a chore but a process that can add real value to the company. It is much more than another hoop that needs to be jumped through or box ticked.

Obviously, as with any new 'process', a real need has to be shown and this can be a hard sell. Often, many of the key people have not been involved in a crisis and again the ostrich syndrome takes over: 'it hasn't happened yet, it may never happen'.

The next chapters cover the processes in detail, from the formation of the team to communicating with internal and external stakeholders. Always keep in mind, however, that the end result needs to be simple and flexible. These are the keys to any successful crisis management strategy.

CHAPTER 11

The Importance of Third Party Advocates

The successful management of a crisis depends on communication. This is self-evident. However, given the intensity of a crisis – particularly in the early stages – it is vital that a company is able to marshal its communications effectively in areas which need it most, not necessarily those that shout the loudest.

Who is this almost silent majority? They are possibly the key people who could leap to the defence of the project or company; however, a good understanding of them is required beforehand. These stakeholders can mean the difference between winning and losing the battle, and you need to know them – well.

But what is a stakeholder in an organisation? The broad definition is an individual or group who may be affected – either beneficially or detrimentally – by the activities of the organisation. Obvious stakeholders include shareholders, employees, local communities and so on.

But today the definition is much wider. Companies are quick to accept that anyone who claims to be a stakeholder in their enterprise must be one. This is a dangerous argument. So, before going any further, it is important to perform some sort of market segmentation – as one would do in any communications exercise – in those who claim to be stakeholders. For example, is Greenpeace a stakeholder in Shell? Is EarthFirst! a stakeholder of the North American logging industry?

So now one must adopt a broad definition of a stakeholder. This is: an entity either affected by the operations of another organisation *or* one which perceives itself as having an interest in the activities of that organisation for whatever reason.

This definition means that every organisation is potentially a stakeholder of every other organisation and the same applies to individuals. This definition is next to useless, yet it is the one which is most commonly used. It is also the back door by which pressure groups can claim to be stakeholders in organisations to which they are vehemently opposed.

For example, Greenpeace, which is completely and irrevocably committed to the end of nuclear power on this planet, can enter into a dialogue with the likes of the nuclear industry, which is totally and irrevocably committed to the furtherance of nuclear power.

Therefore, as an initial broad segmentation, it is fair to say that there are three categories of stakeholder:

- Those who want the organisation or project to *succeed* for their own benefit: employees, customers and so on
- Those who want it to *fail* so that it no longer affects them: Greenpeace versus the nuclear industry, for example
- Those who really are not overly concerned with the arguments, but who will be affected nonetheless (always by far the vast majority). For example, 78 per cent of French electricity comes from nuclear sources, so every citizen is a stakeholder in the nuclear industry, yet almost none are concerned about it.

What generally happens is that the views of the vast majority of the unconcerned citizens are not heard at all. This is normal and is the way of democracy.

The stakeholder diagnostic

Before we approach people in advance of – or during – a crisis, it is important that we know something about them. We do not do business with total strangers. Therefore, we need to understand the universe in which an organisation operates, so that we can manage it. We need to know who are the key movers and shakers (for and against), what is their past history with the company, who knows whom and many other issues.

The way to do this is through the 'stakeholder diagnostic'. This detailed map is the first step in getting to know and understand the complex and difficult entity that is the organisation's universe.

To a greater or lesser degree, most modern democracies have a fairly open form of government where information is freely available. In addition, there is free press that for the most part is unfettered. These two factors mean that there is a huge amount of information in what is generally called the public domain. Yet this information is for the most part ignored. Even worse, it is not collated into a usable form so that it can be applied.

From information available in the public domain, it is possible to put together a good map – on a number of scales from the macro to the micro.

THE DIAGNOSTIC IS A MAP

There are few people who would think of embarking on a long and complex journey without a map. There are whole shops devoted to maps and getting the right one is important. Here are the main problems with communications maps.

The wrong map. It would seem to be an obvious statement that one should ensure that one had the right map: for example, a map of Spain is of little use if one is visiting Italy. Yet that is exactly what happens in complex issues-related communication programmes. People rely on hearsay, stereotypes and gross misinformation when making decisions. When Christopher Columbus headed into the unknown in search of a western route to India, he and his crew were convinced that the seas were full of weird and wondrous monsters that could devour them.

Old maps. Even worse, they rely on old and obsolete information. The restaurant and hotel guide produced by Michelin in 2000 will have very different listings from the one produced 50 years ago. Things change, people change. Look at political parties: who could have believed that socialist parties across Europe would not only allow privatisation of state industry, but actually actively promote it, as is the case with Renault in France, not to mention the London Underground and Air Traffic Control in the UK. And political maps change much more quickly than restaurant guides.

Maps of the wrong scale. Next, people take a map of the wrong scale. A general map of Europe is of little use if one is going hill-walking in the Alps. So, for example, it is assumed that just because a political party has a national policy on a certain issue, then this is slavishly followed in the regions. Nothing is further from the truth. Political parties are broad churches: one only has to look at the UK Conservative Party's totally differing views on the UK's role within Europe to understand this. In addition, some of the bitterness of national politics dissipates at local level. There are numerous dialogues across the political divide in local politics. Anecdotally, we know of numerous politicians who have better relations with some of the opposition than their own party colleagues.

This background information is vital. Even if it does mean disturbing the placid millpond that characterises most communities, it must be garnered. And in as much detail as possible. On each project, we try to build a careful diagnostic of the field we are working in.

Without getting this information, we will always be on the back foot – we do not 'know' our stakeholders. Of course, merely having this knowledge is not enough in itself – in fact, it is far from it. But without it we cannot even make the first step.

Initially one needs to know who are the key political and other players in the area – they are the movers and shakers, the great and the good. This is all garnered from publicly available information. It should cover:

1. The sitting member of the European Parliament
2. The sitting MP
3. The previous MP if relevant, that is, if he or she is going to stand again
4. The local county council: its political composition and track record
5. The district or borough council: again politics and track record
6. The local ward councillors for both the county and district: their views if known (through, for example, letters to newspapers, and so on)
7. The local parish council or residents association: its leading lights, views on issues and so on
8. Local hot issues: for example the closure of a hospital or school, the need for new roads
9. The local media: its campaigns and views
10. Local groups: their campaigns and activities
11. National stakeholders: trade organisations and so on
12. Other relevant information.

Of course the areas and fields are tailored to the size of the company, but let us imagine that this is a medium-sized company with a number of chemical plants dotted in the south west of the UK. Let us now work our way through some of these areas in turn, to see what a diagnostic might look like. It should be stressed that the following represents 'edited highlights' and is not complete.

The local European Parliament representative (probably equivalent to the Senator in the United States)

Constituencies of the European Parliament are huge – with hundreds of thousands of people in each one. Of course, if the project has a European dimension, then the relevance of the MEP will be proportionately greater. However, for most projects, the role of the MEP is not highly relevant.

It is useful to know the agenda of this person: Is he/she a keen environmentalist? What is his/her view of the trade union movement? And so on. There is one key exception – if the project affects the area close to where the MEP lives. It is only human nature that we should take an interest in that which is most local and it would be folly to assume that MEPs, who have probably risen through local politics in any event, are any different.

The local parliamentary representative or Member of Parliament (equivalent of congressman or woman in the United States)
The same comments apply as above, but the local parliamentary representative will take a much more keen interest in events on the ground. He or she likes to be aware of what is happening. If he or she has represented the constituency for any length of time, he or she will know it like the back of his/her hand as well as all the movers and shakers in all parties.

The role of the sitting MP is important: he or she is the pinnacle of local political thought and their opinions matter. However, these opinions cannot run counter to those who elect them and it is important to remember that the foundation of these opinions lie with the regional districts councils and community councils.

Format of the research

For the fictional MP, we have put together a brief report which illustrates the detail which would be useful before approaching any stakeholder, regardless of status.

The sitting MP – Garry Goodwin (Labour)

Background

Garry Goodwin is the sitting MP for Pretty Town, having won the seat from the Liberal Democrats in 1997. His majority is 3218 (6 per cent), which represented a substantial swing of 13 per cent. The seat is therefore marginal.

The son of an architect, he is 55. He has spent many years trying to get elected to either Westminster or Europe. He contested the elections in Diamondshire in 1984, Mt Ommaney (Euro MP) in 1986, Maidesville in 1989, Grassy Hill (MP) in 1992 and was finally elected to the Commons in 1997.

Garry Goodwin was born and educated in Surrey, before taking a BEng at the University of Ripley. He then joined the University of Diamondshire where he rose through the ranks and was head of the engineering department prior to his election

Garry Goodwin is a member of the teachers' union, the NATFHE. He lists his interests as local government, green issues and developing nations.

For hobbies, he enjoys football, gardening, films and his family.

Parliamentary performance

Garry Goodwin is not one to latch himself onto controversial causes. He cannot afford to upset people. He seldom embroils himself in rows and is a great advocate of 'motherhood causes': schools, school transport, the local hospital and so on.

In his maiden Commons speech, he (like most backbenchers) used a local issue – the need for maintaining the local school (which is under threat of being downgraded).

Given that his seat is by no means safe, he spends much time on constituency affairs; so it is not surprising that he does not have a particularly high profile in Parliament. Given the added factor of his age, he will not be on the list of high flyers. Not surprisingly, he only sits on one select committee on trade and industry.

He voted against the government on changes to the schools curriculum but otherwise he toes the party line.

Environmental interests

Garry Goodwin has recently agreed to speak for the Newts Society in the House of Commons. Given that Pretty Town's pond boasts great crested newts, this is worthy of note. He is a member of Greenpeace, although he does not seem to be active in any campaigns.

The next election

The party will have made it clear that they see his re-election as his prime goal as, unlike some of the other marginals, this is winnable again at the next election. Therefore he will be expected to have a strong constituency focus. His chances of retaining the seat are reasonable. Being the sitting MP gives Garry Goodwin an advantage – he can get things done. In addition, the opposition is in disarray.

At the next election, this seat will be fought bitterly. Both parties will have it on their list of key marginals, which means that it will be given extra resources.

The county council

The next level of power is the regional council. Depending on which country one is in, this power varies enormously. Often this power is historical. For example, Italy only loosely united in the middle of the last century, so still has a strong regional structure where the central government has reduced influence. Hence Italy – despite having a government a year since the war – is prosperous.

The USA has devolved many powers down to state level and further. States can set taxes and behave autonomously. Similarly the federal system in Germany – modelled after the war on the US system – sees high levels of federal power. On the other hand, in the UK, the power of local councils was gradually whittled away in the 1980s by the then Prime Minister Margaret Thatcher.

Although councils have had much of their tax-gathering powers either removed or curtailed, they still have huge influence, and in a project where there is likely to be a substantial community impact, they will almost certainly have the right of veto – often through the planning system.

In many countries, there is a dual system of local government with a county council (department in France or canton in Switzerland) and the more local district councils.

The district council

In regional government, one often finds that power is devolved to the district, borough or city level. In many cases, this is the decision-making body on controversial projects, so it is extremely important that it is carefully analysed.

The parish or town council/commune

Again these vary from country to country, but they are very powerful. In the UK, the parish or town council does not have a statutory role. However, they are always consulted on sensitive or controversial matters. The views of the real local people are listened to most carefully by more senior politicians.

These parishes often cover small areas, and contact with individual factories would be more appropriate than contact from a main office. They deal with local issues from a local perspective.

Often district councillors and, indeed, MPs, will also take part so that they can keep their fingers on the pulse of local opinion. If there are going to be problems, it is here that they will start.

Not surprisingly, getting information in a non-intrusive way at this level is difficult. Parish councils do keep minutes, but generally by writing them into a ledger maintained by the parish clerk. This is the only record! However, local libraries and the 'village notes' pages of the local paper can be informative in this area.

Other organisations

In addition, views should be taken on other local organisations, environmental groups and so on. A look should also be taken into national bodies – trade associations, researchers and so on who may also be interested in the area of operation. These can and should be rallied before any crisis hits.

Newspaper campaigns

Local and national newspapers try to gain an affinity with their readership for altruistic and purely financial reasons. This affinity holds old readers and attracts new ones. Therefore one does need to be aware of recent issues in localities, should the 'crisis' be encompassed by a campaign, for example 'clean our river' would be affected by a chemical spill from one of the local factories.

Stakeholder segmentation

As seen in the case of Monsanto and Greenpeace, the organisation which makes the most noise is seen as the most important and (often) the only stakeholder. However, there are five types of stakeholders:

1. *Dependent stakeholders:* employees, suppliers and so on
2. *Impacted stakeholders:* for example those living near a facility
3. *Unknown stakeholders:* for example those who have not made themselves known
4. *Supporting stakeholders:* subsets of the above three categories
5. *Intractables:* those intractably opposed.

Stakeholder mapping or analysis is useless, however, if it is an academic exercise which is undertaken as a stand-alone research project. Too often, this exercise is undertaken to find out who an organisation's enemies are. This is the worst possible use of this exercise. Of course, the exercise does isolate the intractable stakeholders, but they are only a tiny minority, usually unrepresentative and with their own agendas.

It is important to understand that if the stakeholder segmentation is undertaken to isolate these so that they can be 'dealt with' (in either sense of that phrase), the beginning of the end is near. As we saw, to try to seek consensus with one's enemies is a waste of time – they just want to get close enough to you to kill you.

No, a key objective of the stakeholder analysis is to find those who may be able to help the organisation. This research must be applied to be of benefit – it must be put into action.

In particular, it must be used to isolate the special group we call the supporting stakeholders or third party advocates (TPAs), drawn from each of the dependants, the impacted or the unknowns.

Every organisation can divide its stakeholders into the groupings outlined above. In our experience, this can be a fairly simple and, indeed, enjoyable exercise, consisting of five steps:

1. *Undertake the diagnostic.* The level of detail needed has been outlined in the last chapter. However, the diagnostic is not revealed at this stage. If it was, it would tend to skew the exercise and would – in particular – hinder the coming forward of the unknown stakeholders, who are often critical.

2. *Form a brainstorming group.* The next step is to bring together a group of six to ten people with an independent moderator, who has a working knowledge of the company and can guide and direct the group in its deliberations. It should be wide-ranging and include a number of disciplines. Ideally, it should include:
   - Someone with first-hand, frontline operational experience, especially if he or she has been involved in a contentious issue and has some scars
   - Human resources departments can bring an internal/employee dimension
   - Research and development people (if they exist) can bring a more existential feel which, in its blind rationality, can often bring the group back to earth: the 'facts are facts so what is the problem?' approach
   - Outside consultants (no more than one of these, otherwise they start competing), particularly from the lobbying field
   - Someone fairly senior from the public relations department.

The group should definitely not be more than ten (six is not a bad number), otherwise it turns into a mob and can run out of control. The objective is to get as wide a range of views as possible.

Eventually, this may form the basis of a project steering group which will be dealt with later in the chapter. This initial brainstorming group, however, can – and should – involve people who are well outside the project and may have no other involvement in it after this exercise. This is to ensure as wide a range of inputs as possible.

3. *Stakeholder search.* The moderator asks the group members to name whom they believe to be stakeholders in the company. Each of these names is written on a large piece of card. Post-It notes are too small – it is important that the card can be read from a distance. At this stage, no names are ruled out. The objective is to get as wide-ranging a list as possible. Individuals as well as organisations are welcome and the moderator makes this clear. At the end of this part of the exercise, there should be a substantial number (sometimes many hundreds) of names.

When this phase has been exhausted, the moderator brings forward the key names which have been isolated by the diagnostic. What is surprising is that most of these names mean nothing to the group. They are just a list of names.

4. *Stakeholder positioning.* This is a key part of the proceedings. The group discuss their relative importance – generally from their own experiences, but also from a general standing until consensus is reached.

A good moderator will challenge each assumption and ask for concrete reasons for each categorisation. Only when there is concrete evidence and the entire group accept the categorisation is an organisation or individual labelled. What appears is the lack of knowledge of key stakeholders. Phrases such as: 'I was always under the impression that…' or 'I remember they had a particularly vocal member who gave us a lot of trouble some years ago…' will emerge.

Individuals cannot, unless they are nominated to do so, represent an organisation. So, for example, if a local councillor who was a member of the Liberal Democrat group spoke out against a new road, it would be wrong to assume that all his party was now anti-roads. He may have been speaking in an individual capacity, because it went past his aunt's front door.

5. *Stakeholder categorisation.* The cards are then regrouped into one of the five categories:

- dependent
- impacted
- unknown
- supporting
- intractable

As noted earlier, it is surprising how big the unknown category turns out to be. It is important that this exercise is done openly and that everyone agrees – hence the large cards mentioned earlier.

At this stage, the work is not finished. There are more potential stakeholders who need to be isolated. This forces the group to think laterally and positively along the lines of:

- Who else might be able to help you?
- What other organisations are in the same position as yourself?
- Who are the key individuals?
- Have they always been that way?
- What would be needed to change their minds?
- And many, many more questions.

In this latter part of the exercise the real surprises begin to emerge. Organisations which were not even considered as being relevant suddenly seem like potential friends.

The basic message is not to categorise from past behaviours and always be prepared for surprises. Supporters can be found in the most unlikely places, but they need to be cultivated and this takes time.

The power of third party advocates

Third party advocates have a key role in dealing with the media. In the Brent Spar case, Greenpeace enlisted the help of the German Lutheran Church. This church has a boycotting committee and it decided to boycott Shell's products. This was very powerful – even Shell would find it difficult to take on God. But it also gave an independence to Greenpeace's statements that gave it added weight.

Too often they are ignored by companies for a number of reasons:

- *Reliability:* Large organisations are afraid that TPAs will not say exactly what is required. Of course they won't, but that is what makes them so powerful. Journalists do not want to interview puppets.
- *Control:* Companies like to control all their statements. However, TPAs are not making company policy in their statements. They are free agents.

■ *Availability:* Often an organisation does not know who its TPAs might be and none are available.

Independence

Third party advocates are, by definition, independent. And they must be kept that way. It is particularly damaging to try to coach them or get them to be even more favourable. Ironically, a hint of cynicism or antagonism from TPAs makes their statements all the more powerful. So, the following is strong from a TPA:

> No, I must disagree – this company has taken every possible precaution to miti-gate the damage from its facility. I believe it has now solved the minor problem it had and that all will be well.

However, the following is much stronger:

> As you know, in the past I have been critical of the performance of this company. However, I now believe it is making an honest effort to get things right. But, it is early days and we should wait and see. To attack it now just when it is getting its act together is not helpful and one must doubt the motives of those doing so.

The second statement is far more powerful. It is more cautious and less sycophantic – but then that is exactly what makes a good TPA.

TPA IN BRENT SPAR

At the height of the *Brent Spar* crisis, something strange happened. Off his own bat, Tony Rice, a professor at the Institute of Oceanographic Studies, wrote to *The Times* to say that he believed that, rather than causing any environmental damage, the *Spar* would be quickly colonised by sea creatures who would find it a welcome home.

Speaking on a BBC programme after the crisis he said:

> Greenpeace were overegging the cake. They were suggesting disposal of the *Brent Spar* in the deep sea would cause severe damage. Even if the effects were increased by two, five or even tenfold, my point of view would remain unchanged. *Brent Spar* is a small deal.

Unfortunately, that was the last that was heard of him. Imagine if he had maintained his campaign, or indeed – and more importantly – was encouraged to maintain his campaign. Professor Rice is a powerful third party advocate and one that Greenpeace would find difficult to attack. Imagine also if he got his professional institute – comprising many other scientists – to support his position. Now there is a force to be reckoned with.

Analysis

Organisations are far too willing to fight alone. Allies must be sought. Even the world's greatest superpower – the United States – sought allies in the recent Iraq War. Although in terms of fire power, it probably did not need countries like the UK and Spain to fight beside it, in perceptual and political terms, it was essential.

Checklist for identifying your stakeholders and TPAs

As we have said throughout this chapter, it is vital to identify your stakeholders and forge relationships prior to a crisis occurring. The following checklist should help you to do this.

Factor	Yes/No	Action
1. Have you identified all your stakeholders – including suppliers and politicians?		
2. Is the company aware of its local community and political surroundings?		
3. Has the company undertaken a political and community diagnostic in order to do this?		
4. Has a brainstorming group been formed to identify stakeholders?		
5. Has the brainstorming group completed a stakeholder segmentation exercise, categorising stakeholders into A, B and C groups in terms of importance to the company?		
6. Have relationships with key stakeholders been forged prior to a crisis occurring?		

Conclusion

TPAs are generally not helping a project from a profit motive; often their involvement is altruistic although, of course, they may have their own win–win projects. They can speculate openly and even inaccurately and the Law of the Absolute does not bind them. So, to the question, 'Do you think this plant is absolutely safe?', they can answer 'yes' without being stuck with caveats.

Like journalists, TPAs must be cultivated well in advance of the crisis. However, well-placed, well-informed and articulate TPAs can have a powerful role. They can certainly defend and promote the company strongly.

CHAPTER 12

The Crisis Management Team

Putting together a crisis management team (CMT) is one of the most important aspects of forming effective crisis management procedures. Without an effective team, which works well and understands its role, procedures and planning mean nothing. Choosing the team is a key part of the strategy, mixing depth, knowledge and leadership.

When a crisis hits, managing it is like managing a destroyer in a sea battle. At sea, when a battle is imminent, the captain calls 'battle stations' and everyone must move to preassigned roles. In such a situation, if people do not do exactly as expected – moving accurately and quickly to their own stations – then the battle risks being lost.

This is not the time for thinking. Thinking is dangerous. All ad hoc manoeuvres must be stopped. The person who decides – even with the best of intentions – to override the overall plan and take independent actions is a danger to him/herself and his/her colleagues. There is a bigger picture and this must be adhered to precisely.

This is a time for callousness. When teams of explorers attempt to climb Mount Everest, there is an honour code which says that those who cannot make it are left behind to die. It is the only way to ensure the safety and lives of the majority of the team. By helping those who are too weak to help themselves, not only are you endangering yourself, but also the rest of your team. This is exactly how it is in a crisis. You must stick to the plan, even if immediate events are dragging one towards a different activity.

So, for example, if you have been delegated to contact the local mayor and the telephone rings with a call from CNN, demanding an immediate comment, you will stick with your plan. You will give CNN the number of the press office and quickly and politely hang up. Certainly CNN is important, but there are others to deal with as well. It is not your job now. And the local mayor is important too. After all, CNN will move on, the local mayor won't.

Setting up a crisis management team

Navies have had many years experience in putting together their action plans and setting battle stations. Nothing is left to chance. A battle is a crisis and the navy prepares carefully and makes sure that it is as ready as possible; after all, that is its job.

Even though most countries are almost permanently at peace, the navy is still busy. It organises exercises and manoeuvres to test itself in battle conditions, sailors and officers are trained as to their roles in battle and everything is in the highest state of readiness – waiting for the next crisis when they can be called upon at any moment.

Like the navy, a modern corporation does not just have a crisis to deal with, it must also get on with its business. However, the same principles still apply:

1. Each person who is involved in a crisis must be assigned a role.
2. No person should take on another person's role.
3. Each person must be fully equipped to handle the role correctly and precisely.
4. Each person must be tested in the role.
5. Each member of the crisis team must be aware of the roles of the other team members.

Assembling the team

Any crisis management team must be easy to assemble. Reactions will need to be quick. In general, it should be possible to assemble the team within an hour. In highly sensitive industries, such as chemical or aviation, this period is probably 30 minutes.

This has practical implications. The key members of the crisis team – and it is a condition of entry into the team – must live within reasonable distance of the crisis management centre. They are of little use to anyone if they are stuck on a motorway.

Duplication of roles

Murphy's Law says that a crisis generally strikes on the last holiday weekend of August. Therefore it is important that all roles within the crisis team are duplicated – and in some cases triplicated – to allow for holiday and sickness. The practical implication of this is that, for example, the crisis management team leader (CMTL) and the deputy CMTL cannot take holiday at the same time and must coordinate their diaries.

Given the importance of this key role, if the CMTL goes away, then the deputy should appoint someone else to take on the role of CMTL in the event that he or she should not be available.

This is onerous on staff, but then a crisis is like war – it is a tough place and preparation is everything.

The crisis management team's key roles are:

- To make key tactical, operational and strategic decisions
- To clear information for public use
- To manage the support teams.

These roles are considered in more detail later in this chapter.

Reflecting the navy, each member of the CMT should look to separate roles within the team, so that each person has their own responsibilities and procedures during the crisis. This is to ensure that the team runs efficiently, rather than risking the same tasks being duplicated, or, worse still, not done at all. It is also a time for ruthlessness. If a person, no matter how senior, does not have a specified role, then he/she should not be in the team. Again, this is often easier said than done.

The role of the CEO

The best place for any CEO to be when disaster hits is away from the office, in public and at the epicentre – be that outside the headquarters or at the scene of the crisis. It is here that the full strength of the CEO can be put to good use. The diagram on the next page shows a typical crisis management team.

What needs to be understood is that there are not just the technical factors but also emotional factors involved in a crisis. People respond to emotion; after all it is a very human response to any situation. In a crisis situation, facts and figures mean nothing and arguments cannot be won or lost on this ground. This is something that many companies forget.

During Johnson & Johnson's Tylenol crisis, with the concerns over possible contamination by a blackmailer of its products, the then CEO Jim Burke publicly apologised and announced the decision to pull the product from shelves. This human and moral response helped put a face

Structure of a
typical crisis
management team

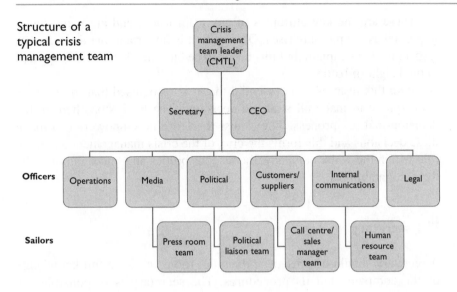

behind the brand and showed that the company put people first. This was something which the general public, somewhat jaded by images of corporate greed, could relate to.

To this end, the CEO should report into and be guided by the crisis management team.

The crisis management team leader (CMTL)

As with any ship, there can only be one captain. Again, using the navy analogy, the most high-ranking admiral is subservient to the ship's captain whilst he is on board that captain's ship. This is how it must be in a crisis.

In the crisis management team, this is the crisis management team leader. Those with experience of sailing – even in the smallest boat – will immediately recognise that there can only be one leader. Regardless of whether crew members are unsure of a decision or strategy, they do not stand and argue – they follow. Removing or second-guessing the captain at the height of battle is madness.

Debate obviously plays an important role, as in any team, but the time for debate is before the crisis, not during it. In these crises, however, there is no time for a 30-minute discussion to precede every little action; the larger strategy – yes. However, the smaller details need a large amount of trust, leadership and vision.

These are the key attributes of any team leader and are increasingly important as the pressure rises. Obviously it is important that the crew has respect for their captain, but this needs to be built in advance – not queried in the height of battle.

With this in mind, it is essential that it is recognised that the leader's main role is to make all strategic decisions. The buck stops here in the decision-making process. They must therefore be empowered to make these decisions and this forms the crux of the crisis management team, the role within the wider company, the responsibilities and, more importantly, the accountabilities.

The secretary

A secretary should be present in the crisis room and have full knowledge of the company and its procedures. The secretary is responsible for logging every event during the crisis. Members who leave the room should inform the secretary of where they will be. In general, the secretary to the crisis should be the secretary of the crisis management team leader. It is important that they have a close working relationship.

The secretary can also fulfil the role of butterfly – a role which is outlined in detail in Chapter 13.

The officer cadre

Beneath the leader – or CMTL – in ranking order, will be the officer cadre, those who are trusted to advise on the decisions that need to be made. This is generally a team of five or six people where each is assigned a specific area of responsibility.

This is common not just in the navy, but also in all walks of life. It is their job to gather, interpret and filter the right information, reducing the noise that can strangle the process, suffocating decision makers with useless facts and irrelevant situations.

They will work closely with the leader by facilitating actions and decision making. A key role of the officer is to make sure all actions are implemented and maintain a constant information flow with the remaining members of the crisis team as well as the chief executive and board members.

Whilst each corporation is different, the following generic areas are common to most, and should act as rough guidelines for the distribution of responsibilities within the officer cadre:

- Operations
- Public affairs
- Media
- Internal communications
- Customers/suppliers
- Legal.

Operations

The role of the officer with responsibility for operations is to ensure business continuity and that all business operations are adapted in light of the crisis. We touch further on business continuity – which should run almost parallel to the crisis team – in Chapter 19. However, regardless of whether this consists of a fully fledged business continuity team or backup outside the crisis management team, the operations leader must liaise with these bodies and ensure that the crisis does not interfere excessively with operations.

The media

The officer in charge of the media must liaise with reporters, organise press releases and news conferences and ensure that those who are handling external calls from the media, such as in a press room, are fully updated at all times. It is key that this person has wide experience in handling the media.

Public affairs

This role will mainly entail liaison with the political community and pressure groups and ensure dialogue with key politicians and stakeholders. Again, during a crisis situation this can become a heated role and needs to be reflected in the individual chosen.

Internal communications

Employees are the ambassadors of the company and the officer with responsibility for employees must ensure that employees are kept updated and informed. He/she must also ensure that there are sufficient personnel to aid the crisis team. For this role, some consideration of existing human resources staff may be worthwhile, as they have an idea of internal issues, company structure and dealing with employees.

Customers and suppliers

Maintaining the reputation of the company is a key priority during a crisis. Ensuring solid and consistent customer service is therefore crucial. The role of the officer with the responsibility for customers is to converse directly with large customers and ensure that the call centre is fully updated and operating at the correct capacity for customers to access it.

Legal

The role of the lawyer in a crisis is to ensure that the company acts, operates and makes statements that are legally correct. A secondary role is to ensure that the company does not make commitments which might, in the future, damage it.

Maintaining and managing responsibilities

As there will almost definitely be overlap between each of these sectors, it is essential that each is keenly aware of who is handling what and the extent of their remit and responsibility. By far the greatest problem in a crisis – and it happens all too easily – is mixed messages. Slight variations are quickly seized upon by opponents and turned against the company. Even when the same message is interpreted by two different people, if this is then expressed in two different ways to the same stakeholder, the result is a very confused stakeholder. Mixed messages reinforce an image of confusion and incompetence.

Certainly, there may be other emergencies – or events – which happen during a crisis which are not directly relevant to any particular role and, if they are relevant, they must be assigned by the CMTL to one of the officers. It is vital that each person retains their preassigned role throughout in order to achieve consistent messaging.

Creating a strong crisis team

It cannot simply be assumed that once a crisis team is appointed it will be able to operate effectively. This is not the case. Boundaries need to be defined.

Most thinking on crisis management in recent years has stressed the importance of having a crisis team and identifying the roles that are needed within it. However, establishing the responsibilities for the team members alone will not ensure that the team is a *good* team.

As any chef knows, getting the right ingredients is only the first step in a recipe. The next step is to ensure that he has the right mix – otherwise it is quite easy to end up with a finished product which is too spicy or too bland.

It is a truism to state that teamwork is vital in meeting the challenges faced during a crisis. However, many companies have examples of teams which are disorganised and where personalities clash. This effect is heightened in the pressure cooker situation of a crisis management room and can quickly become an explosive combination.

It is therefore totally unrealistic to assume that, with the additional stress generated by a crisis, the team will suddenly be able to operate in a seamless and high-performance way. On the contrary, the normal breakdowns that block team performance are exacerbated by the crisis.

The following are some problems common to crisis teams. A key objective is to ensure that the team is strong enough to weather the storms ahead.

Working to the same goals

In a crisis management team, there will be representatives from a number of different departments from within the business, from legal to operational, security to financial, each with their own interpretation of what is right for the company.

In the normal, everyday running of any business, these departments may come into conflict with one another – operations managers feel the firm should be spending more on high-quality components, marketing departments think that more should be spent on advertising and typically finance feel that there should be less on both. All, however, probably believe that their solution is the right, and possibly the *only*, one that will maximise profit and be the best for the company in the long run.

In a stressful crisis environment, representatives from these departments not only have to work in close proximity but have to make crucial decisions concerning the future (and at times survival) of the company, and it is in these situations where conflicting viewpoints come to the fore.

A particular example of this conflict is that between the legal and public relations department. Stereotypically, the legal department will want to take the cautious approach and say as little as possible. The public relations department will want to say as much as it can, to kick the issue out into the open, and inform the media, customers, consumers or the community. The PR department knows that during a crisis the vacuum of information created by a lengthy silence can potentially cause more serious consequences than any financial or legal ramifications. This is where preparation comes in. The PR and the legal department should role-play a number of crises as part of their training. It is from these that the lifebelt statements emerge (see Chapter 15). These pre-prepared statements can easily and quickly be modified to give a rapid response to key audiences.

In general, the first response by the team should be to collectively sit down and work out this response and then rapidly agree on priorities.

Working together

Because of the smokestack nature of today's corporations, it is possible that those within the team have never actually worked operationally with one another before and will therefore have different views and attitudes. These will naturally be brought into the crisis room and can affect operations and decisions within the crisis team.

During crisis management training, rather than during the crisis itself, one should establish all the team members' understandings and values. Crisis management training is an excellent method of team building (see Chapter 18). The focus needs to be on building trust and for each team member to get to know his or her colleagues and their strengths and weaknesses and, most importantly, accept them.

It is dangerous to simply assume that individual values and expectations will be shared by the other team members. This is rarely the case even if they do work for the same company. Structures will help to keep this in check.

Who should be in your team?

Stress and emotions can run high during a crisis which, if not properly understood and channelled, can naturally lead to a negative effect on the team's ability to make decisions and solve problems.

The environment that a crisis creates means that team members' personality traits are likely to be accentuated and enhanced. What is easier to control in a normal working environment is less easy to manage when time is limited and the decisions are of paramount importance. Tension, the emergence of internal company politics and disagreements can therefore emerge within the team. They have no place in the team and must be managed out before the crisis.

Therefore, it may not *necessarily* be the heads of divisions who take on the roles of the chief advisers or the officer cadre. Although it is certainly likely that at least some of these will end up in the crisis team, their ranking within the company alone is not enough to justify this. For example, the head of a division may have an important operational role, which means that he or she is more valuable elsewhere. The selection process has to be based on the person's overall value to the company rather than routine position in the organisational hierarchy.

Important questions need to be asked of people in order to determine this. Will they fold under enormous pressure? Are they willing to work around the clock to get the job done? For many people, do they understand that a crisis situation needs be handled differently from routine work and are they willing to learn and learn quickly? These are the key elements of a good crisis team member.

It is the responsibility of the leader to decide who the members of the team should be and, here, he or she must be as ruthless as a football coach or manager. As always, the leader's word is final.

Choosing a crisis management team leader

The CMTL must have the following key personality traits:

■ *Authoritativeness:* The CMTL needs the respect of the other crisis team members and the workforce. In a crisis, which is an unsettling time, the leader must give assurance that the crisis team is in control and acting in the best interests of all concerned.

- *Decisiveness:* Difficult decisions will have to be made within a short space of time. A company needs to be seen to be acting during a crisis and acting quickly.
- *Ability to communicate:* The CMTL needs to be a first-class communicator in order to get important messages across to the team and others quickly.
- *Diplomacy:* Although as leader and captain, the CMTL has absolute power, he or she will use this with discretion and tact. Otherwise, the team will be broken and, in the worst cases, a mutiny may occur.

The officer cadre

The officer cadre needs the following key traits:

- *Communication skills:* The other members of the crisis team must also have excellent communications skills in order to:
  - Communicate messages quickly and effectively to the other officers
  - Filter important information to the CMTL and the chief advisers
  - Get messages through to those outside the team, both internally and externally
  - Converse with important stakeholders and delegate tasks to internal departments.
- *Discipline:* The officers need to know when to provide assistance and backup and when to implement changes to the plan. They must work with the CMTL, however, and should not act unilaterally and risk the overall plan. Once decisions have been made, they must not be second-guessed.
- *Commitment:* A crisis is an intense period in which the intensity will undoubtedly increase rather than decrease. The officers need to be able to go into autopilot and be highly motivated from the start and maintain this until the end.
- *Team players:* The importance of teamwork has already been stressed. The officers need to be cooperative and work on building relationships rather than causing confrontation.
- *Decision makers:* They are the CMTL's chief counsel and need to be fast thinking in helping him or her make vital strategic decisions. They cannot therefore be 'yes men', but must strike the balance between working together with the CMTL and being relied upon to speak up when they feel changes are needed or the wrong course of action is being taken.

■ *Be responsive:* As we will learn in Chapter 13, the CMTL and the officers will need to react quickly to information provided to them.

■ *Be able to look at the wider picture:* The officers must each provide specific expertise, but each must also be able to take into account the whole perspective in relation to the company.

■ *Be calming:* They must be able to stay calm, remain as unstressed as possible and remember that their job is to alleviate the concerns of the CMTL rather than add to them. Their role is to provide counsel rather than additional problems. They must be practical and logical.

■ *Be able to delegate:* Decisions made by the CMTL and the officers must be filtered through, implemented and facilitated effectively.

Checklist for establishing the CMT

Before you move on to form support teams or the next stages in preparation for crisis management, use the checklist below to help you to see what actions you need to undertake in order to establish your CMT.

Factor	Yes/no	Action
1. Is there a crisis management team?		
2. Have roles been identified and assigned within the team?		
3. Is each person fully equipped to handle the role correctly and precisely?		
4. Is each member of the crisis team aware of the roles of the other team members?		
5. Do the team members work well together?		
6. Is the team robust under pressure?		
7. Is it easy to assemble the team?		
8. Are roles duplicated in the event of team members being ill, unavailable or on holiday?		

Information flows: the support teams

As noted earlier, the key roles of the crisis management team are to take key decisions, clear information for public use and manage the support teams. In order to be able to fulfil this function, a calm and considered atmosphere is essential, as is an appropriate flow of information.

When a crisis strikes, the amount of information (not to mention questions) generated is enormous. In the days before email, everyone got on the telephone to ask his or her colleagues what was happening. Result: information gridlock. Today, it is even worse, because with email, one can send a message to hundreds of colleagues with the click of a mouse.

From the outside, the pressure can be enormous. As we will see in Chapter 15, the media watches the media. Go to the office of a national newspaper news editor and you will find a bank of TV screens, with CNN, BBC, Reuters, Bloomberg and so on. If a story breaks on one media, then it will be relayed around the world in a matter of seconds. This in turn creates an avalanche effect and the media queries come piling in.

Obviously, all this information needs to be managed. This is a key role for the support teams.

For example, in a crisis including an operational element, the information is first scanned by the filtering room (manned by operations managers) and key information is then fed into the crisis management team. This ensures that only the key facts are passed on. This information needs to be logged (more on this later) before being considered by the crisis management team. If a decision is made to act on the information, this can be taken in a calm and considered manner.

If the company's public statements need to be modified, this can be completed and the new statement passed to the support teams, media, public affairs and so on. This is the role of the butterfly, which is outlined in Chapter 13.

Checklist for establishing and preparing support teams

The checklist below will help you see what actions you need to undertake in order to establish your support teams.

Factor	Yes/no	Action
1. Has a press team been established?		
2. Has a political liaison team been established?		
3. Has a call centre or sales manager team been established to handle all other queries?		
4. Has a human resources team been established for internal communications and operations?		

Factor	Yes/no	Action
5. Have separate and adequate rooms for the CMT and support teams been prepared which are in close proximity to one another?		
6. Has each been supplied with the adequate equipment?		
7. Is security adequate?		
8. Has a filter room been established?		
9. Has a 'butterfly' (see Chapter 13), a member of the CMT, been appointed to liaise between the CMT and the filtering room?		
10. Has a secretary been appointed to record the crisis?		

The roles and operating environments of the CMT and each of the support teams are considered in the next chapter.

Responsibilities and Logistics

It is of little use telling a journalist from a major national TV channel that the reason he did not get a response to his query was due to the fax machine being broken. Or telling your local mayor's constituency office that the phone call went unrecorded and therefore the question raised went unaddressed.

Everything is intensified in a crisis. Time constraints are greater. There is a huge increase in internal and external communication. The decisions that are made take on a whole new level of importance. Throughout all this, accuracy and consistency are of the essence, otherwise mistakes will happen. A suitable environment is paramount, because it is all too easy for the smallest of mistakes to allow the crisis to escalate and spiral out of control.

Watching five directors of a major multinational company fiddling with a broken photocopier for fifteen minutes was undoubtedly one of the most amusing crisis incidents I ever witnessed, but during a crisis is not the time for your senior management to have to worry about resources. It sounds simple, but one of the most vital things you can do in preparing for a crisis is to ensure that you have adequate equipment and it is all in working order. The crisis room and the press room should be big enough to include all equipment as well as giving those present plenty of room to work.

Ensure that there is a checklist of the equipment that each room will need and ensure that the electrical equipment is regularly checked. The list should include the following items:

- Landline phones with numbers that are not widely disseminated so they cannot be tied up
- Computers with Internet access and electronic whiteboard facilities

- Fax machines
- Television, radio and video to monitor the media
- Flip charts and whiteboards.

There should be a stationery cupboard and a photocopier nearby.

As well as what to include, it is equally important to know what to ban entirely from all rooms used by the teams, and the single most important is mobile phones.

In the previous chapter, the structure of the crisis management team was outlined. Here we look to their specific roles and responsibilities

The Crisis Management Team (CMT)

In a battleship, the area from which all major strategic decisions are made is the bridge. The bridge is not filled with 22 officers and 37 crew members. Generally it has a small number of people within it – the captain and a few others.

Similarly, the room from which all major decisions are made should consist of no more than seven people. This should be the CMTL and the officers, as outlined in Chapter 12.

Responsibilities

The crisis management team has the following main responsibilities:

- Making all major strategic decisions
- All communications including:
  - Updating the press team and call centre, and supplying the content of external messages
  - Internal communication and delegation
  - Communication with top level politicians
  - Communication with head office, parent companies and major shareholders
- Keeping the CEO fully updated
- Ensuring business continuity
- Making approvals relating to budget and so on.

The hymn sheet

The CMT team is also responsible for preparing, agreeing and seeing to the distribution of the company's statements or hymn sheet to the support teams. There is more on these in Chapter 15, but each should be numbered, timed and dated, no matter how they are distributed.

Equipment

As the crisis management room is a place for decision making and information dissemination, not a huge amount of equipment is needed. What is required is now outlined.

An electronic whiteboard

The crisis room team should have regular updates on the progress of the crisis and decisions that are made. This will ensure that new information is not misplaced and that internal and external statements remain consistent and up to date. Therefore decision sheets need to be kept, which log every decision made, the time it was made and who authorised it.

These can be kept on an electronic whiteboard attached to a computer with a printout facility. Team members can focus on the crisis without having to make individual notes and everyone receives the same information, with no miscommunication or omissions.

Three computers with printers

One computer is used by the secretary and the others are for general use. Many PR people, for example, cannot work without a computer. The computers should have an email facility with a separate account name and be used primarily for outgoing mail.

Telephones

The exact number will be determined during training (Chapter 18), but if everyone has a telephone in a small space, then no one can hear and chaos results. Therefore three among the team is probably enough. The numbers should be only disclosed to a small number of people in the support teams.

Mobile phones are banned. Each team member should leave these with their secretaries who can filter messages as they come through.

Fax machine

Although fax is rapidly being overtaken by email, it is still important. Murphy's Law says that when you want to communicate with the prime minister, that is exactly the day that the email won't work, but the fax will.

The butterfly

The role of the butterfly can be taken by the secretary, but this depends on the scale of the crisis and how busy the secretary is likely to be. The butterfly is part of the CMT.

Responsibilities

The key role of the butterfly is to disseminate information and decisions. For example, communication between the crisis management room and the filtering room should be by this individual. The butterfly also ensures that key decisions and updates on the company's position are passed to the other support teams, for example, the press office. The butterfly is probably the only person to leave the CMT room during the crisis. Again, with email, even this may not be necessary.

The filtering room

The number of decisions to be taken is few, but it is important that they are taken with the best possible information available at the time. In a crisis, a huge amount of information is generated and much of this is of little value. However, there is a real possibility that important information can be either mislaid in the rush or obscured by sheer volume. Therefore, a mechanism for filtering information needs to be put into place.

Responsibilities

In the diagram in Chapter 12, the filtering room reports to the operations director, which assumes that the crisis is an operational one. This room deals with information coming inwards and going outwards. Every ship has an engine room and, in a crisis, it is the filtering room which serves this purpose. It is occupied by a maximum of five to seven people from the next tier of management in the operations division.

The team in the filtering room is responsible for:

- Updating the crisis management team
- Filtering the requests of the crisis management team through to the various departments and divisions throughout the company
- Passing down through the operations part of the company the various decisions made by the CMT.

Equipment

The equipment in the filtering room is similar to that in the CMT's room and includes:

- Electronic whiteboard
- Computers
- Telephones (mobiles are also banned here)
- Fax.

The filtering room should be located close to the CMT, ideally next door. This is not so that members of the filtering room can visit the CMT, who should be left in peace, it is so that the butterfly can move paper-based information quickly.

The press office

Chapter 15 deals in detail with press relations. This section puts the press function in perspective with regard to the others in the crisis management team.

The press office is going to be a busy place in a crisis and a customised and separate room should be pre-prepared. No one from the press office has access to the crisis management room – it is already represented on the CMT by its officer.

Responsibilities

The press team is responsible for keeping all the media informed. As with all public statements from the company, the same one is used for all audiences: media, politicians, employees and so on. The press office will also decide on which interviews to grant, arrange press conferences and ensure that statements are placed on the website.

To ensure that information given to the press room is not duplicated or that messages do not conflict, only one person from the crisis room – the butterfly – should feed press statements to the press team. Naturally, the press office will communicate with its CMT media member so that he or she can input into the strategic decisions being made by the team.

In a major crisis where there are thousands of calls, others may be drafted in to deal with media queries. These need not be skilled press relations professionals, but they should be trained to stick strictly to the hymn sheet and not stray from it. Whilst this may be frustrating for journalists, it is essential that the company maintains a line and is not drawn into speculation. For the journalist, the result may be that some information is better than no information and this often suffices.

Equipment

The press office should be in a separate pre-prepared room with a telephone and computer for each person. Mobile phones have to be allowed here, as a competent press officer will ensure that he or she has good contacts in the media and that they have his or her mobile number. However, there is a case for the mobiles being given to a secretary and again messages can be filtered.

A notice board on which statements and printouts from the CMT's whiteboard can be pinned is useful.

Political liaison

Many companies may hold the dangerous assumption that because the crisis does not have a direct political impact, it is of no interest to politicians. Politicians are interested in everything that affects their constituents. After all, they have been elected to *represent* them.

Responsibilities

The political liaison team is responsible for keeping key politicians informed of what is happening. This should be done on a proactive rather than reactive basis. Politicians hate to be blind-sided, especially where their constituents' welfare is concerned. The answer 'I don't know' is not popular with elected representatives; it is their business to know.

Pretraining of key managers is essential. Again, it is vital that managers stick to the hymn sheet, but with the politicians who are known to the company (and they should be), managers should have some leeway to open up – without any wild speculation – in order to engender trust and maintain their relationship.

Equipment

This team can often work from their own offices once a robust means of getting the hymn sheet to them is in place.

The call centre

Responsibilities

Presuming that the organisation has a call centre or some form of sales centre, this is an ideal place from which to handle all customer calls and calls from members of the public. Again, they must stick to the hymn sheet and not – under any circumstances (as they don't know who is on the end of the phone) – be dragged into any speculation.

Equipment

Presuming that the hymn sheet statement can be sent by email, the call centre can operate as normal. Given the large volume of calls, however, it may be wise to set up a separate free phone number to handle crisis calls. This should have a prerecorded message.

For example, when electricity companies have power cuts – due to storms or the like – useful messages go as follows: 'We are aware that there has been a power cut, but supplies should be restored by midday.' This satisfies most people's need for information and keeps the call centre free.

Employees

As well as being sound management sense to keep one's employees informed during a crisis, they can also be important ambassadors for the organisation. It is not helpful to have an employee telling the media, if they are suddenly asked: 'To be honest, I haven't a clue what is happening.' The role for keeping staff informed usually falls to the human resources department, and this is covered in greater detail in Chapter 16.

Responsibilities

To ensure employees are informed of the crisis and the company's response to it. Again, they will work from the hymn sheet.

Equipment

There is no particular need for any special equipment and, working with their respective CMT member, this function can be performed from regular offices.

Contact record sheets

Contact record sheets should be kept for all contact from the media, share-holders and politicians. They should be laid out as follows:

- Personal details including name, organisation, contact details, who spoke to them and at what time
- Issues and questions raised during the conversation
- The response that was given
- Further actions.

This should be kept simple, as shown opposite.

Distribution of statements

As noted above, one of the key responsibilities of the CMT is to prepare, agree and arrange the distribution of statements and information. Statements

Contact record sheet

Journalist Name: *Joe Smith, regional reporter*

Organisation: *CNN*

Telephone number/email address: *01234 567890,*

joesmith@cnn.co.uk

Mobile (evening):   *07771 234567*

Date: *1/1/2000*   Time: *2:13pm*

Contacted by: *Anne Brown, Press Team*

Issue/Questions:

What are we doing to ensure the safety of the community?

Is it true that there is cyanide in the river?

All the fish are dying, what are you doing to save the fish?

Has heard it will take up to a year to completely flush the system of toxins. What do we plan on doing to address this?

Our response:

Apologise for what has happened, as of yet not ascertained whether the contamination is cyanide, however, we are doing everything possible to identify the cause and are working closely with the local authorities in an emergency clean-up exercise.

Further actions

Prepare media response, spokesperson from company to speak in 6 o'clock news slot relating to the most common crises should be prepared in advance so that they can be released immediately. Update statements can then be prepared every 30 minutes, if the crisis has evolved or more frequently should there be a need.

Some statements, however, can be pre-prepared and these should be cleared with the legal department, again in advance. These are called 'lifebelt statements' and this is a typical one:

> We are very much aware of our customers' concerns and we are working hard to resolve them as quickly as possible. We work very hard to try to ensure high standards. However, we accept that some customers are dissatisfied with our service and we offer our apologies and will correct circumstances where we can as soon as possible.

This gives the press office and others a holding statement with which they can begin to give some comment rather than remain silent. As with all statements, this draft must be cleared by the CMT even though it is fairly anodyne. It is then distributed by the butterfly.

All statements should be maintained on an electronic whiteboard attached to a computer with a printout facility and they must be consistent for all audiences.

Security

Tighter security is needed during a crisis. The company can still remain open, friendly and caring through its external responses and the decisions that it makes regarding its employees, stakeholders and the media. In particular, front reception needs to be strengthened and the crisis area needs to be sealed immediately.

Conclusion

No matter how prepared you are or how organised your company, during a crisis Murphy's Law not only rules, it takes on a life of its own. What can go wrong will go wrong, and if it doesn't, it will soon. Therefore, the better the environment is to deal with unforeseen eventualities, the easier it will be to tackle these eventualities head on.

CHAPTER 14

The Crisis Management Handbook

The crisis management handbook should never be viewed as an instruction manual for each individual emergency or crisis situation. Nor should it be a record of every intricate detail, procedure or evacuation plan of the entire corporation, spidering into a myriad of teams, groups and subgroups to such a point that, in a rushed situation, the right information is there but cannot be simply accessed or understood. It is in such situations that too much information is almost worse than no information at all.

The crisis management handbook should be a simple pool of information which can be relied upon to provide accurate guidance. The general principle within the team, that each member has an area of responsibility, is reflected in the handbook. Therefore responsibility devolves to each member to ensure that data are kept accurate and up to date. This mechanism maintains these documents and ensures that they remain current and also short.

There are a number of crisis management plans sitting on shelves of businesses across the world that have not been read.

The principle behind a crisis management handbook is that it should be easy to read, easy to use and simple to understand. The last thing any team needs in a crisis is a vague knowledge of 'something in the crisis handbook somewhere' which can be misinterpreted in the heat and pace of the crisis situation. The best model for a crisis management handbook is the phone book. It is useful, referred to frequently and is simple to use.

When was the last time anyone read the phone book cover to cover? However, did this stop it from being useful last time a number was required? The answer is clearly 'no' to the latter – and hopefully 'never' to the first. The phone book is laid out in such a way that the information needed is directly to hand, quickly available, easy to reference and in a form that can be taken and used within seconds – no interpretation required.

This should be the form of any successful crisis management handbook, not commentary, reams of regulations and procedures, but succinct, important information which is relevant and useful to any crisis. The objective is to do the donkey work now, when the time is available to complete what can often be an onerous paper trail, so that it does not have to be undertaken in a situation where time is short and nerves are frayed. In essence, the handbook is an essential stage of preparation.

Obviously, the contents of crisis management handbooks vary from company to company and can come in a variety of shapes, styles and formats. The most successful ones have one common attribute – they are short. They do not need to be books, but more like a collection of leaflets pulling together information from across departments and the business.

It is essential that the handbook is easily accessible, but not, for obvious reasons, openly available. There should be a current copy in the crisis room. For those on the move, the handbook should be available securely on the company's intranet site.

Layout and style

The layout of the crisis management handbook is clearly something which has to be individualised to the company, and contents will vary, but the basis and the ideas behind the contents are fairly standard. After all, any good crisis management handbook does not address the crisis situation, but gives the tools available to help to tackle it.

Again, it is important to stress that each section should be short and to the point. Why write a paragraph when a bullet point will do? Do not explain the obvious and use as few words as possible. These books are produced as a directory and an aide-mémoire, rather than a comprehensive book intended to teach the process from scratch. Hiding details in long, lengthy paragraphs and carefully explaining their existence are not needed. For example, the paragraph above could be displayed thus:

1. Keep each section short and to the point.

In essence, the handbook must be short, flexible and useful. The contents of the handbook should mirror the roles of those who play a key role in the crisis management team, and they are given the responsibility for keeping it updated.

Content

This section is a 'rules of engagement' document. It doesn't need to be, and shouldn't be, a weighty or lengthy part of the document. It should, however, include points on:

- How to use the plan
- Basic tips on managing the crisis
- The remit of the crisis team.

Forming the crisis team

This section should simply describe how the crisis team is initially manoeuvred into action. A central point of contact is needed and telephone numbers, contact names and details should be included to ensure that the team can assemble quickly and easily.

Procedures

This page should contain what is a basic outline of the crisis procedures and how the team works. Again this should not be long and lengthy – reflecting points rather than passages. It should set out:

- The rooms, teams and roles
- Agreed contacts and mechanisms for distributing information.

Roles

This section of the crisis management handbook should look at the tools required by each of the roles, tailored not just to the area of responsibility but to the individuals charged with this role. This not only focuses the mind but cuts down on bureaucracy and ensures that the documents produced are genuinely useful and relevant. The roles already covered earlier in the book are:

- The crisis management team leader
- Operations
- Public affairs

- Media
- Internal communications
- Customers/suppliers
- Legal.

A general page should first set out the members of the team, their substitutes, their departments of operations and all contact details – including home address and telephone numbers, pagers and mobile telephones. These are key pages which bring the team together at the given location.

For each of the roles, the corresponding page in the manual has to have a number of points to ensure that communications run smoothly. Suggested content for these pages should be:

- Agreed role and area of responsibility
- Telephone numbers and contact details of key contacts within the department and area of responsibility
- Key details relevant to their particular roles.

An example of what to include is shown below.

Public affairs

Names and contact details for:

- Local council information and structure (leader and so on)
- Local politicians covering the area(s) of operation
- Key national contacts representing area of work and operation
- Local residents and action groups
- Contacts at key local and national newspapers
- Internal press office resources
- Lifebelt statement.

This key section will be referred to during the crisis for details, resources and contacts to call on for support.

Telephone directory

The phone numbers, direct lines, mobile numbers, faxes and email addresses of all team members should be listed. Also included should be key members from outside the team who may be required to step in during the crisis. This simple step can save a huge amount of time searching for details and can be easily updated by human resources or a similar department on a regular basis.

There should also be a separate list of key customers, suppliers, regulators, authorities, the media and so on, listing almost every business they may need to call on. In addition, there should be a short listing of useful numbers of local services such as hotels, pizza delivery, bus lines and so on.

Checklists

All good processes require a good checklist. Forms can be a chore in everyday life, but in a crisis, they have a vital role. Firstly, they direct and guide the user to input information which is directly relevant. Secondly, they make it easier to process, as all the correct information has been gleaned.

In a crisis situation, this is very important. The crisis team needs to make decisions and communicate them. It needs the right information and time taken to extract this, or reference it, takes time from these core objectives. The role of the crisis management team is not to process data, but to act on it.

As with all lists, an external eye is always useful. These checklists should be agreed by the whole team, as often additional input can be sought from those outside the sourcing department.

A typical checklist may look something like this.

Assessment
1. *Identify and have an understanding of the situation*
2. *Ensure staff and workplace safety*
3. *Determine if additional support is needed*
4. *Call upon crisis team, and support for team*

Crisis team remit
1. *Assemble in crisis rooms*
2. *Core team:*
   - *Confirm roles within team*
   - *Review facts and form key messages - timeline*
   - *Consider strategy - including outside support*
   - *Notify external stakeholders*

- *Develop and distribute information*
- *Begin media interactions*
3. *Work with stakeholders and employees:*
   - *As knowledgeable sources of rumours*
   - *To convey information*

Company-specific information
1. *Designate resources/communication mechanisms for the following:*
   - *Stakeholders*
   - *Employees*
   - *Customers and suppliers*
2. *Identify a crisis team liaison member*
3. *Provide services as needed*
4. *Distribute appropriate information/aid*

Review
1. *Review the actions of the day:*
   - *Hourly reviews of crisis intervention activities*
   - *Identify weaknesses and strengths of crisis interventions*
   - *Review status*
   - *Prioritise needs and personnel needed for the next day*
   - *Plan follow-up action*

These checklists are vital, so it is essential that time and energy are put into these areas beforehand to ensure that actions relevant to each individual company are minuted and processed for action. For example, a chemical factory may have to secure the premises and inform government agencies during a fire, which is a different course of action from that required in the case of an office block fire.

In a more general sense, checklists for procedures within the team should be short and rarely call upon members outside the crisis rooms.

Contact record sheets

Within the team, each member has a number of areas of responsibility and
a number of contacts. In the crisis management handbook, there should be
forms to keep records of contact and ensure that actions are caught. A
typical layout would enable the form to be filled in by hand – often easier
to fill in when on the telephone and making calls. Or it can be computer-
based which is often easier for distribution by email.

The header of the form should incorporate contact details and administration areas to allow the form to be filed and used effectively. Although
this seems like an administrative chore, and unnecessary, the team needs to
be able to find all information logged rather than hunting in notebooks and
piles of paper. The details that need to be included are:

- Name of contact
- Team member
- Time/date of call
- Contact details for further contact.

The following headings should take the remainder of the space, with the
majority set aside for the contents of the contact:

- Aim of call – key messages
- Summary of conversation and points made
- Actions and next steps.

The contact form then needs to address the reason for, or aim of, the
call (did the stakeholder call the team or did the team initiate contact?) and
also the content of the message. This is purely for consistency and to
ensure that the team can be updated with other members' contacts.

One of the most important parts of any contact record sheet is the
actions and next steps section: were there any actions promised? Was a
further call required? These must be captured and followed up. By doing
this, these reports can be faxed outside the team, if possible, and a
complete picture of the contact can be given and acted upon by those not
part of the core operations (for example sending off to a key stakeholder a
copy of the press release or annual report). As outlined in the previous
chapter, contact record sheets should look something like this.

Contact record sheet

Name of contact:

Team member:

Date of call: Time of call:

Contact details for further contact:

Telephone number: Email address:

Mobile (evening):

Aim of call – key messages:

Summary of conversation and points made:

Actions and next steps:

By keeping accurate records in a way which is useful to the team, these reports help in managing the crisis and also drawing learning from it.

Background material

As part of the handbook, it is important that there are some facts, figures and information which can be drawn upon in a time of crisis. This is not the place to fill pages with corporate brochures or information which can be obtained from general documents. This is for real facts and figures: company turnover; number of employees; information on processes used by the company. It is also the place for additional information on details listed on the roles pages.

For example, background material could include notes on key media and politicians, background to the area, sample press statements and so on. This section is less of a directory and more of a brief guide to the company and key statistics.

Format of the handbook

The crisis management handbook – once the information has been compiled – has become not just an important document, but also a sensitive one. There is information here that identifies both strengths and weaknesses. Therefore it is important to ensure this is recorded and treated as such. Clearly, a crisis management plan needs to be easily accessible and there are a number of formats it can take. The most obvious is a book format, or ring binder, which ensures that it can be frequently updated in part, rather than new documents issued every time a telephone number is changed.

With modern technology, a number of businesses are moving to electronic versions and there are obvious benefits. An electronic format allows much more information to be placed, easily referenced and searched through. The temptation, however, can arise to produce too much – simply to fill a space.

Secure Internet sites are clearly a good format for the handbook, provided Murphy does not make it crash! In a crisis, human nature dictates that one turns to what can be trusted and easily referenced – paper. Many believe that email has cut down on paper consumption; however, important documents are always printed. Therefore it is key to the design of any electronic web page that the whole document can be easily printed and used as a paper version.

Electronic versions do offer one useful benefit – they can be easily updated with minimum effort, so ensuring that all members of the team always have the most recent document at their fingertips.

In reality, most people tend to use both electronic formatting and paper, so it is best to have both available.

Distribution and updating of the handbook

A key role of the handbook is not only to give direction, but to give help. Frequent testing of the crisis management procedures can ensure that it remains updated and – essentially – remains useful to the process. As previously mentioned, once the plan becomes bulky or outdated, it becomes irrelevant to the process. Updates should be produced regularly, probably monthly or even quarterly. Again, this is a simple task, but ensures that the information is current.

After each test, the handbook should be updated to reflect any learning points or additional contact which was helpful. If paper copies are produced, new versions should be signed in and out, to ensure that each member has handed back previous copies and received new ones. Obviously, each is numbered with a version number.

Checklist for writing the crisis management handbook

Writing your crisis handbook need not be a daunting task. You can use the following checklist to help you prepare and ensure that your handbook serves its purpose in your crisis management preparation.

Factor	Yes/No	Action
1. Does your company have a crisis management handbook?		
2. Is it easy to read, easy to use and simple to understand?		
3. Is it no longer than 25 to 30 pages?		
4. Does it contain concise sections on: – forming the crisis team – procedures – roles – public affairs – and a telephone directory with all important internal and external contacts?		
5. Does it contain simple checklists on: – assessment – crisis team remit – company-specific information – reviewing?		
6. Does it contain contact report templates to record all contact with relevant stakeholders?		
7. Does it contain background information and statistics about your company that are relevant and useful in a crisis?		

Conclusion

The handbook is very much a tool and should not be seen as a restriction, or something that pushes aside the creativity or problem-solving of the team. The aims of the handbook and checklists are simply to be resources, a mind jog or a best practice guideline. Overall, in the production of the handbook, it is necessary to ensure that this is kept in mind.

CHAPTER 15

Managing Media Relations

If one looks at the impact of external communications, then the channel with the greatest impact is the media. It is instantaneous, independent and universal. From newspapers to TV and radio and now the Internet, the media is everywhere. As noted in Chapter 6, the media sets the agenda, it acts as magnifying glass on tiny details and it is relentless.

Therefore, whilst other audiences – politicians and regulators – are far more important in their long-term effects on a company, they will also take their lead from the media. No one wants to be associated with trouble and the media can make trouble.

Getting the message right

One of the most important pieces of advice that can be given regarding external communications in a crisis is to be prepared.

The lifebelt statement

The press release (see below) is useful for print media as they can take direct quotes from it. For broadcast media, however, it is also useful to have a key sound bite prepared, which, of course, is exactly the same as that which appears in the press release – it is just an extract.

This key message is a lifebelt statement, which interviewees can use if they get into trouble on the key benefits or defences (if bad news) which are contained in the release. Politicians are masters of this. Their rule is: Always answer the question you had hoped you might be asked. A company in crisis cannot be so cynical, but it is important that you get the message across, even if one is being led down a different path.

A sample lifebelt statement could be:

> Let me assure you that this company is doing everything it possibly can and that we are working closely and openly with the authorities to solve whatever problems there may be. It would be wrong of me to speculate, but we are doing everything in our power to find the answers.

The lifebelt statement does not have to be long, about 20 seconds is an ideal length for a sound bite for a news programme and so on.

Questions and answers

A common ancillary to any media statement is the question and answer sheet. This is a useful exercise which looks at all the difficult questions that might arise from the issuance of the press release.

Most public relations departments can produce question and answer sheets to cover the most difficult questions. These can also be read carefully by a spokesperson before an interview.

The Q&As attempt only to cover potentially contentious issues. The questions are deliberately framed in an aggressive way – such as one might get at a raucous public meeting. They do not cover basic facts that can be gleaned from published information. They should not run to more than two pages, otherwise they would not be properly assimilated or used.

The Q&As should form a consistent hymn sheet from which there is no deviation. Answers should be formulated in such a way as to make them specific, but also broad enough to be used as statements for other questions.

There are some fairly simple rules surrounding these Q&As:

1. They should not state the obvious facts – they should only deal with that which is contentious.
2. They should not take up more than two pages of A4 – if they run to more, you should reconsider whether you actually really want to send out this release at this time. If it is raising more questions than it is answering, it may be fundamentally flawed.
3. They should not contain any 'land mines'. In other words, there should be no facts buried within them which are not evident from the press release. There is no room for being economical with the truth.

These key messages and statements should be consistent and should be used for *all* audiences, not only the media. Inconsistency is the great failing in most crisis management programmes. Get it right once – and the media are the toughest audience – and then repeat the message for everyone else.

Crisis preparation for the media

Too often, crisis preparation is almost totally internal and this is often the case with the media. This preparation is obviously important and is dealt with later. But much can be done in advance of a crisis. For example, it is common sense to state that we all work better with people we trust and trusting someone means knowing them. Yet it is amazing how few organisations make the effort to get to know the journalists. They have not built relationships on trust.

As part of any crisis preparation, a programme of journalists' briefing is essential. Ideally these are best done as one-to-one meetings to get to know journalists on a personal as well as professional level. Naturally, journalists are slightly cynical when first approached. Therefore, it is important to have a story or at least a suggestion of a story to bring to the meeting. The company need not write this story – particularly not in the press release format – in advance of the meeting. This more informal approach allows the journalist to come to the story rather than having it thrust upon him or her. In this forum, a press release can be seen as threatening. In addition, if the meeting occurs over lunch, and the press officer is buying, there is a hint of bribery.

Initially these meetings are best undertaken by a company press officer, who will often be a former journalist. If this works well, other initiatives can be undertaken with the same journalist.

The chief executive

There is little doubt that by far the best PR person in every company is the chief executive. This is not because of his or her communications skills, but because journalists like to get as near the top as possible to give greater credibility to their stories.

Therefore, one-to-one briefings with known journalists and the chief executive are very fruitful. Ideally, these should be undertaken without the presence of a 'minder' in the form of a press officer. Brief the CEO well and then trust him or her. After all, when something has been said, it cannot be unsaid so the minder has no real role.

Obviously, other members of senior management can also undertake this role but they are never as powerful as the CEO.

Media training

Today's media can be very tough and there is little mercy shown to an organisation in trouble. Therefore, as with any military training, those who are to face the media must be subjected to the sounds of battle. This is media training.

For key spokespersons, such as the chief executive, a full-day, one-to-one session is recommended, with refreshers every six months. Certainly, this is time-consuming, but then what is the company's reputation worth?

For others, half-day sessions in groups of three are adequate. Obviously the session is recorded and analysed. The best sessions work with a real journalist, who breaks the training into three phases:

1. *Knock them down.* This is particularly for those chief executives who are used to getting their own way and who often surround themselves with yes men. A good frightener from the journalists sets the tone. It is wise that as few people as possible witness this.
2. *Build them up.* The second part allows the participant to become familiar with the media, prepare answers and understand the danger of the situation.
3. *Build confidence.* The final sessions show how to be prepared, treat the media with respect and hold one's ground in a confident and non-arrogant way.

Dealing with the media

In general, one interacts with the media in three ways:

- by press release
- by interview – in person or by telephone
- at a press conference.

Press releases

Without doubt, the sooner a company in crisis gets out a statement, the better. Even if this statement is anodyne and fairly content-free, saying something is better than saying nothing. At least it shows that the company is aware something is happening to which it should react. This statement can be built upon as the crisis evolves and be posted on the Internet, which makes it easy for journalists to use as it can be cut and pasted.

As the company wants to show a human face, the press release should contain quotes from a senior person, but not the chief executive in the early stages. There is too much uncertainty and one does not want to lumber the company figureheads with something which may be damaging later on.

However, as a crisis evolves and reaches a plateau, the press release can run into a number of problems:

- *Lack of continuity:* For any communication to be effective, it needs to be intensive. For example, TV advertisements are repeated many times in order to have the desired effect. The problem in a crisis is that, after the first few press releases, they run out of things to say. In addition, by its very definition, news is new. Newspaper editors are not in the business of rerunning stories.
- *Journalistic cynicism:* In addition, these releases are viewed cynically by journalists. As well as 'they would say that, wouldn't they', there is a lingering impression that an organisation is only releasing good news and suppressing bad news. This is particularly so if the organisation will not put up any spokespersons for interview. It looks like one is hiding behind the release.
- *Door opening:* Never open a door that one cannot shut. A press release is a public document and puts the company in the spotlight. Is everything else in order or will the release just cause a number of other awkward questions to be asked? For example, you have fixed this plant, but how about the others which are still subject to further crisis?
- *The legal department:* A press release is effectively a statement of company policy. Therefore, it will have to be vetted by a number of people, not least the legal department. (If your legal department is not vetting your press releases – well, good luck – you now have a real problem.) These cautious folk can very quickly emasculate a strong press release into nothing. In a crisis, this is of little use to the journalists.

The impact of the release

When one is dealing with a crisis, the mere fact of actually sending out a press release is a significant event in its own right. But the impact of the press release as it lands on the journalist's desk is difficult to gauge.

The journalist may decide on a number of courses of action:

1. Put it in the bin – often the least dangerous from the organisation's point of view.
2. Check in the cuttings library to see what has happened to the company previously. In this case, the organisation must be aware and be ready to defend everything that has happened in the past.
3. Call the opposition to get their views. The press release can then be turned on its head, with the protest or green group getting their message across instead of the organisation that issued the press release.

The use of the release

However, press releases do not have the same level of control as that offered by advertising. One has to allow another individual – this time a journalist – to alter the content before it can be used.

There is one sure fact about the press release: it will not be used verbatim. (Of course, certain media will often take advertorial and use text exactly, but they usually demand advertising support – which, in effect, makes it advertising by any other name. Other lazy media will use it verbatim, but, by definition, these types of outlet have no clout and are useless.) And, as noted above, if the journalist is any good, he or she will need balancing comment, but in this case it is to balance your arguments and counter them.

A useful exercise is to role-play the journalist in one of the media you would like to have use the press release. Then judge the likely reactions – what will he or she do when they get it? If you do not know the answer to this, you are effectively walking in the dark with a hand grenade, with the pin pulled out in your hand.

Then attempt to write the story as they might write it. As noted, most organisations have ex-journalists in their PR department, so this is a fairly simple exercise. However, it may not be a pleasant one. When the finished article is passed around senior management, it often tempers their enthusiasm for using the press as a mechanism of influence.

Using the press release in a crisis

If you have bad news to announce to the media, the best way to do it is through route one – the direct, open and honest way. Put the news up front. In addition, do not drip feed bad news. The company which announces that it had a small leak of effluent gets some bad headlines on the day. However, if that leak – after investigations by the regulatory authorities – turns out to be 40,000 litres, then it is another bad story – how the company tried to cover up the original 'small' leak.

One or two strong, honest press releases at the beginning of a crisis – like the opening moves in a chess game – often determine the outcome for the company.

As always, many variants must be prepared in advance and they *must be cleared by the legal department in advance*. Otherwise nothing of any real meaning or value will emerge.

Interviews

The chief executive should be the face of the company during the crisis. However, although he or she is a primary spokesperson and a key one, he or she should not be the sole spokesperson. The fact is that some chief executives are brilliant businesspeople but not very effective in-person communicators. This doesn't matter for written communications and may not matter for some audiences. As identified in the previous chapter, in many instances the mere presence of a chief executive to show the 'caring' and 'human' face of a company is enough.

However, in a major crisis, one person cannot be everywhere and several other spokespersons will be needed to speak to the media during press conferences, in interviews and in important meetings with key politicians and stakeholders. Developing a list of qualified personnel in different areas of the organisation who could serve in this role gives flexibility of response. Perhaps some are from the crisis team, but this will have to be carefully judged: after all, the crisis team's role is decision making and information dissemination. It might be as well not to distract them from their task. Certainly the press office and its members have a role here.

Image communicates as strongly as facts, as politicians know well. You only get one chance to make a first impression. It is estimated that 58 per cent of the impact made is down to appearance; a further 35 per cent to tone of voice and only 7 per cent to the words actually used. So in the words of the Canadian media pundit, Marshall McLuhan: The medium is the message. And you must choose this medium carefully, so it is extremely important to choose the right spokesperson.

As is often the case, it is easier to pick on those types one should not choose rather than those who might just be right for the role. There are certain types of people who, though capable and probably excellent in other areas within the company, are not suitable as spokespersons for the company:

- *Zealots:* 'I am great, the company is great and we have done nothing wrong.' Zealots are those who believe that the company and what it does is fantastic. Most senior members of a company will contain elements of this within their working persona and this is naturally commendable within the business, as it shows loyalty and motivation. The only problem with zealots is that no one believes them. They may appear arrogant, as if they are avoiding the questions, in dealing with the public and the media – thereby projecting an image of a 'suit' who talks only in 'PR-speak'. By injecting technical jargon and refusing to apologise during a crisis, the company's biggest advocates can be lethal.

- *Loose cannons*: They can be members of the public or a pressure group and here they have a valuable role for these organisations, as speculation is great media fodder. But they make dangerous spokespersons within an organisation. Key personality traits in loose cannons is that they do not think before they speak, are unpredictable and do not respond well to stress. They may therefore project an air of insensitivity on behalf of the company. Since you are never sure what loose cannons may say under stress, it is best to keep them out of the spotlight.

- *Honest Joes:* Honesty is the cornerstone of effective crisis management, and honest Joes have their heart in the right place. An honest Joe feels compelled to tell the truth, the whole truth and nothing but the truth in the most sincere way possible – including the most confidential of internal information. However, honest Joes may fail to understand the importance of the proper response at the proper time, expressed in the proper manner. In that way, they resemble loose cannons.

- *Timid Noras:* Some personalities are not meant for the spotlight even though they are some of the most highly qualified people in the company. Scientists (and two of the authors come from this background) often fall into this category. Timid Noras feel intimidated by close questioning or confrontations. They act nervous and upset; they may even feel guilty. And, in the media, if you look guilty, you are guilty. They do not make effective or credible spokespersons.

So, what type of person does make an effective spokesperson?

■ *The straight shooters:* This is a person who has a deep understanding of the media and the mindsets of journalists. Many will have been former journalists. They know that flannel and whitewash will not work. They are confident without being arrogant; diffident without being weak; open without being injudicious; friendly without being overfamiliar; calm without being complacent. They are also rare.

It is important that these people are in place, trained and ready to step into action. This credible face is 93 per cent of the image – and the reputation – of your company.

What should be said

The most important thing to remember in a crisis is that if you do not speak up for yourself, then – unless you have prepared very well – no one else will. It is hard to make friends when you are down. Politicians are quick to take sides – usually with the underdog not the big corporation. Remember, the vacuum caused by a failure to communicate is soon filled with rumour, misrepresentation, drivel and poison.

Facts are always scarce and the truth is an early casualty. The real facts – when they emerge – do little to wipe out the perceptions that have been created during the crisis.

The media have no obligation to report the facts: conjecture and wild speculation make far more interesting and entertaining topics. But you are constrained – you must tell the truth. Do not tell lies or speculate. It will always come back to haunt you. Remember Bill Clinton. Every sensitive document will be leaked – treat all information as being public, it will come out – probably sooner rather than later.

If you are interrupted (even unfairly), do not interrupt back. The interviewer will lose audience sympathy and you will gain it. Speak slowly. If you are a rapid speaker, slow down. Try it with a Dictaphone – we all speak too fast.

During a crisis there are no better words than 'please', 'thank you' and, above all, 'sorry'. Even if you have prepared the longest, most factual of explanations, it is these words which will speak volumes.

The interview environment

It is important that the interview is conducted in a calm and quiet environment. One cannot have the hubbub of the crisis in the background. Remember, perceptions are everything and if it looks like chaos, people will assume it is and nothing anyone says will overcome this.

If the media is to come to you for an interview, pick either a quiet room – do not use corridors – or an outside location, which often looks better, where you will not be disturbed. If the media is to turn up at the company's headquarters, a secure meeting room on the ground floor should be prepared so that they can use this as a base.

Press conferences

The world of the press conference is changing, with the emergence of the Internet as a major new dissemination medium. Nowadays, a company can easily post a media statement on its website and that will satisfy the needs of most journalists.

However, a press conference is a good way of disseminating a substantial amount of information in an open and fair way. It also has the secondary benefit of showing that the company is willing to face its public in a transparent way and be questioned about its problems, plans and intentions.

It is extremely important that external comments are consistent. In a press conference, you must be sure of the facts, ensuring that everything stated is accurate and justifiable. This is not the time for speculation, it will be seen as a cover-up further down the line.

Here are some basic guidelines for a press conference.

Security

The press conference room must be secure. If it is held at the company's headquarters, the names of all invited journalists should be given to the security at the front gate. Those who turn up – and are not on the list – should be met *at the gate* by a press officer. If they are authentic and not members of an activist group, they should be allowed to attend. If the press conference is not held on company premises but on neutral premises such as a hotel, security – although much more difficult – is important. However, if activist groups make enough fuss, it is difficult to exclude them. The mere act of exclusion can escalate the crisis even further, particularly if there is any suggestion of manhandling.

Registration

Ensure all journalists are registered as they enter. Journalists should enter by one door, company personnel by another and they should leave by the same doors. This is to avoid impromptu press conferences where journalists try to pick off-the-cuff comments.

Chairing the meeting

It is important that the press conference is tightly chaired, with agreed terms of reference set out at the start by the chairman. For example, he or she may say that the company will present its information and all questions will be held until the end.

Length of the press conference

The best rule here is: as long as it takes. Trying to truncate a press conference is a form of hiding. It is best to have all the questions and get everything – as far as possible – in the open.

Timing

There is not much point in having a press conference if there is little to say. Therefore it may be some time, maybe 24 hours, before a normal press conference is held. Of course, there will be interaction with the media in advance of this, but a press conference needs careful preparation and thought, given that it is a public examination by a group of journalists in front of – often live – TV cameras.

Frequency

In a major accident crisis – such as the Swissair crash (Chapter 1), press conferences were held daily. This was a useful way of getting information into the public domain. Also, journalists knew when the next press conference was scheduled for and this took pressure from the company.

Company website

A section of the company website should be put aside for the media. The media should then be alerted that statements will be posted on this website. Obviously, some media will forget about this, but they can be quickly directed to it in the event of a crisis. This has the advantage of giving a fast response and also, for print media, the benefit of a cut and paste electronic statement.

Conclusion

The media is a powerful means of disseminating information. It should be used for this purpose. However, it can also be extremely damaging and it is important that a company prepares and trains well for dealing with the media. Others will be taking their lead from it.

CHAPTER 16

Internal Communications

In a crisis, as the outside world begins to attack the carefully crafted brand and company that has taken years to painfully build up and nurture, you forget your friends. In particular, one set of friends that are much more loyal to a company than you may think – the employees.

To ensure that they have the right information and are able to join you in defending the company and its reputation while working through the crisis, a process has to be put in place to ensure that everyone has the same message and the same information, regardless of whether they are internal or external facing.

Most companies make great play of what a valuable asset their employees are – hence the term human resources. But, in a crisis, when events are moving quickly, employees can end up like the cuckolded husband – the last to know. The target is not simply to pull the company through, but to make sure you bring everyone along with you. This is the reason why internal communications are important. What is a company without its employees? For internal piece of mind and consistent external messaging, internal communications need to be effective.

The rumour machine

Mushroom management – keeping employees in the dark and pouring manure on them from time to time – is not acceptable. Yet, even the best companies tend towards this extreme in a crisis. Who cares about the fitter in the maintenance department when the reporter from CNN is looking for an interview? This can have a huge impact on morale and staff motivation. The company will – one hopes – continue after the crisis. These well-motivated people will be very important then.

If internal communications is sidelined during a crisis, the next best communication mechanism – used by offices and companies all over the world – will take over. The system is effective and is the modern day version of the tribal drum – office gossip. In the absence of anything else, it will become the communication that will be trusted and relied upon by employees. The space left by a lack of information is filled by rumours – and this is also very much the case with internal communications.

The water cooler becomes less of a utility and more of an opportunity to discuss the latest events and trade the recent titbit of information gleaned from their work. This can be damaging for a number of reasons:

1. *If you hear the same thing enough times, it becomes the truth*
   In the absence of any other direction or information, repetition breeds fact. If the same misinformation is heard from a number of sources, it is deemed to be true. In a time where it is crucial that there is consistent and honest messaging, this can be potentially damaging while the company works through the situation.

2. *If no information is being conveyed, something must be seriously wrong*
   If there is no flow of information, people assume that the company is in such serious straits that they must be hiding information and hence speculate as to the extent of this.

The gossip chain is clearly a damaging and obvious complication and hence the flow of information is not interpreted by the usual rumour mill.

There are, of course, other advantages to good internal communications. After all, it is key that the right hand of the company is well aware of what the left hand is doing so that resources can be carefully managed at a time when the company is often stretched.

Means of communication: email and web pages

The most obvious form of communication is through the Internet and intranet and by email. This is by far the most effective form of communicating to large bodies of people. However, caution must be used and the information carefully balanced to provide as much information as possible, whilst being aware that whatever is distributed is likely to end up in the public domain at one time or another. Again, the same key messages should be delivered from the hymn sheet. Treat them not as press releases but on a par with them.

Email groups in this situation are useful and important. Emails should be sent regularly, but not so often that they create more work and less benefits can be drawn from them. A useful time period, in the early hours of a crisis, is every two hours. Any longer and the rumour mill will fill in the gaps. They should be sent to everyone, with the provision that it is simply an internal update.

However, the internal communications manager and the crisis team itself should be very much aware that with one click of a button, the email could appear in a local or national newspaper or be distributed worldwide. UK government adviser Jo Moore found this out when she noted in an email that the aftermath of September 11 would be a good time to 'bury bad news'. It was soon all over the newspapers. In effect, there is no such thing as 'for internal use only'. Everything is in the public domain, so treat all missives as if they were going to Reuters.

With this in mind, any email and other such communications noted below should be plain in style, spin-free and as practical as possible. For example:

Update: 11:43 3/5/04

As you might now be aware, there has been a suspected effluent leak reported in the River Fleuve, which is speculated to have come from one of our plants on the riverside, namely the Diveneago plant. We are testing, independently, the water and investigating the effluent from the plant. It is worth noting that there are five other plants which may have also caused this, and they are also doing the same.

While this testing is happening, there may be questions and so on from customers and from other stakeholders. If they would like any further information, patch them through to Jane or Steve on *4483.

We have a team looking into this, and will keep you posted. If, however, you would like any further information, please email info@supacleaninc.com or give Gary a call on *8656.

Messages should include the following points:

■ Time of last update
■ Current understanding of situation
■ What the company is doing about the issue
■ The company's views on the situation

- How it is handling the media (optional – depending on intensity)
- When the next update can be expected.

All this information is not just useful, but is important in ensuring that it stops misinformation from spreading and it also reduces the divide between management and employees.

Web pages

There are, of course, other ways of quickly disseminating information. Staff-only web pages, or web logs, are a useful way to communicate for those who may be dotted around the company. But remember that the warning given about email also applies here – everything is in the public domain.

These can be a focal point for more frequent updating, and useful for those where sending an email would be a disruption and drain on resources. Web logs act almost like bulletin boards – a central page where information can be exchanged. Such web logs have successfully been used in a number of different areas to ensure updated information is exchanged in an easily accessible location. For example, the US presidential primary candidates effectively used the technology to motivate supporters and ensure that those working on the campaign were up to date with the latest statistics and information. This was an incredibly effective and time-saving way to ensure that, in a frantic situation, one action can update a number of people.

In the short term, when the focus of energy is predominantly on tackling the issues, these instantaneous methods of communications work very well. A key role is not to feed too much information so that the situation becomes confusing, but to quench the thirst for information.

Written communications

In a crisis, the more traditional methods of internal communication, such as staff newsletters, monthly meetings and the slow filtering of information through management structures, are useless (in any event, for the majority of companies, the company newsletter is an organ that is produced in good faith, but rarely read). In a crisis, because messages change so quickly and lead times are so lengthy, the newsletter would be redundant before it is printed.

The CEO's letter

However, there is a role for thoughtful and timely written communications in a crisis. Ideally, this should come from the CEO and should be individually addressed. Again preparation is essential here – of envelopes, addresses and so on. But, given the nature of the communication, this is not the cover all, chest-thumping newsletter, but a thoughtful letter explaining exactly what is going on – from the hymn sheet – no deviation. It explains the company's position, what its next steps are and the importance of the employees at this time.

Notice boards

If all staff are based in a central building or concentrated into a certain area, a less technical way of spreading information is to have a central whiteboard or notice board to which information such as press releases or more general update information can be posted. This is a less effective way of spreading the information, but it can be put together quickly and if placed near a common place of entry or gathering area can be an effective way of keeping people generally updated with the details.

Personal contact

There is nothing like a face-to-face meeting. No matter how useful, email is impersonal and – like all written communications – open to misinterpretation, depending on the mood of the recipient and the sender. British Airways has – over the years – often had stormy relationships with its employees. In the delicate business climate of 2003, a crisis in the form of a strike could have ruined the company.

BRITISH AIRWAYS

In July 2003, British Airways was hit by a wildcat strike. The company was forced to ground all its flights from Heathrow Airport's Terminal One. Close to 90 flights were cancelled after baggage handling and BA ticket staff walked out en masse, leaving 10,500 passengers stranded while it was estimated that around 100,000 were affected in total.

The strike was in response to BA's plans to introduce a swipe card entry system which employees would have to use. Ostensibly it was designed to enable managers to monitor employees' working hours. Employees, however, feared that this would enable managers to send employees home during quieter periods and call extra staff in at short notice during busy periods. This new system was imposed on BA staff after months of negotiation had not addressed workers' concerns.

British Airways' brand rested on how quickly it could reach agreement with the unions. The company had already been hit by the global economic slowdown, the impact of the war in Iraq, the post 9/11 effect and the recent outbreak of SARS in Asia. If that were not enough, in July BA announced pre-tax losses of £45 million for the second quarter of the year. This dispute could not have come at a more critical time.

The threat of strikes continuing through the summer would have been potentially devastating for BA. After 10 days of talks, the Chief Executive Rod Eddington stepped in, meeting each of the union leaders in person. He quickly brokered a deal and the strikes were called off.

Analysis

Although better internal communications would have prevented the problem turning into a crisis, BA did act relatively quickly. In terms of the crisis curve, Rod Eddington stepped in after the crucial point where the crisis kicks into life. However, he managed to prevent the crisis turning into a disaster. The point of no return was avoided. This meant that whilst BA was damaged and could never return to how things were before the incident, the company was nevertheless able to return to a similar position.

The relay team

The crisis team will not have time to deal directly with staff – even those in their own divisions. The relay team provides a useful firewall between employees and those dealing with the crisis.

This internal communications body, usually up to four people depending on the size of the company, can be chosen in advance; often they may be PAs or secretaries who will pass on only what they have been given and will not speculate or gossip.

This may seem like a cumbersome task with an unnecessarily large organisational structure. However, given that the majority of employees will be happy simply to be told what is happening by email, calls to the relay team should be minimal. It is an important firewall that can stop rumours from starting and gives a good indication to the internal temperature of the company. The structure and its interaction with the crisis team are expressed diagrammatically below.

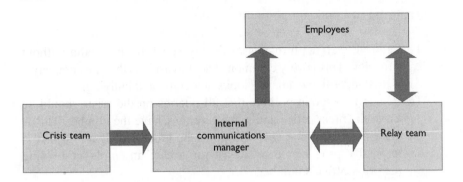

It is important that the majority of employee contact goes to the relay team, leaving the internal communications manager to take an overall view of the situation and plan strategy. Getting the message right is just as difficult internally as externally. The relay team should produce reports on any feedback, of which there should be little if the correctly tailored information is distributed. Any information should aim to satisfy curiosity rather than drown it in detail.

Internal communications and the media

In the world of the Internet and 24-hour television news, communication to employees – if not done by the company – will be done by the media with whatever spin they care to place on the information. Therefore, press releases should be available to members of staff, so that they may also keep abreast. These should not be circulated as a matter of course, but made available perhaps via a website, web log or internal resources folder/mechanism. This will ensure that staff can see what the company's viewpoint is. However, this is not force-fed, as workloads should not permit too much information to be digested.

Staff contact with media

A key question often asked by employees is: 'what should I do if I am approached by the press?' This can easily happen outside a factory gate, for example.

There are two options:

1. Threaten all staff with dismissal if they speak to the media without authorisation. This is very common. The downside is that the company – when it is under fierce attack – looks autocratic and bullying.
2. Train staff to respond politely that all queries on the crisis should be passed to the press office and make sure they have the number. This is far more preferable and also will never be broadcast. It would take a desperate TV producer to broadcast footage of an employee reading out the press office's number.

After the crisis

For longer term issues, clearly the focus can shift to internal communication mechanisms with a different slant. More use can be made of traditional methods such as newsletters. However, they need to take into account a balance of facts and also that they will be seen in the public eye. Wider and more public displays of strength and loyalty can be taken towards staff, ensuring again that you bring them along with you.

Good examples of this can been seen at a wide number of multinational companies where employees remain informed during long and drawn out processes such as those described in Chapter 11, where companies in the US can spend months in a technical and restructuring limbo while complicated proceedings are taken by a small number of individuals. Companies such as WorldCom and ntl – both previously hugely successful telecom companies – have emerged from these proceedings. Employees have to be kept informed and involved with the proceedings.

Following a crisis, the internal communications manager needs to fully brief the existing internal communications team in a handover session (if he is not already a member), with agreed objectives for any further communications set by the crisis management team and messages again set by the team. The crisis team, following the intense action of a rising crisis, will still need to tidy the remains of any particular event and it is through these actions that the internal communications team can play a role in ensuring that employees are not forgotten on the road to recovery.

Further initiatives, for longer term strategies, may involve debriefing managers, who can then in turn debrief their employees. This should never be used as a method during the crisis itself – it would almost be a case of Chinese whispers, and just as damaging.

Once the crisis has passed, a further letter from the CEO or chairman is appropriate. Again, this should be straightforward, honest and spin-free. This alone can give a great boost to morale, and is so easy to do yet often overlooked.

Checklist for internal communications

The checklist below will help you to prepare your internal communications.

Factor	Yes/no	Action
1. Have effective communication channels been established internally prior to a crisis occurring?		
2. Are managers and employees kept regularly updated as to events and changes within the company?		
3. Has a relay team been established to convey information to employees during a crisis?		
4. Have web-based and written communication channels been established that can be used during a crisis?		
5. Have staff been trained to handle media and other queries?		
6. Are all the staff within the support teams prepared?		

Overall, internal communications at least have to keep pace with external communications – after all, they are third party advocates in their own right and should be utilised as such.

CHAPTER 17

Managing Politicians and the Public

For a senior politician, not being able to speak with a senior member of the company is insulting. For a key customer, being transferred from department to department causes aggravation. For a journalist, having to wait for an extra half an hour due to consultation needing to take place with a parent company (which leads to a missed deadline) causes frustration. And for the company, all this is extremely damaging to reputation.

Preparation and testing before the crisis occurs is crucial. Are all your links functioning properly? Is information passed through the appropriate channels without the facts being distorted? The crisis team needs to routinely test all networks to ensure that external communication channels are operating effectively, as during a crisis, they must do so.

The politicians

Most large companies have a public affairs department, often supported by consultants, whose role is to provide advice on regulations which may affect the company, lobby on behalf of the company and keep the organisation informed of legislative or other changes which may affect its wellbeing.

As noted in Section B, politicians hate to be blind-sided – especially when approached by media – so it is important that they be contacted proactively rather than reactively.

As always, preparation is key and the crisis management handbook – or a section of it, depending on the sensitivity of the information – should be reserved for key public representatives. It may be that certain phone numbers are reserved for the head of public affairs and his deputy: one does not want the home telephone number of the environment minister in everyone's hands.

Communications at the highest government level

Prior to the crisis, the public affairs department should be delegated the responsibility of pulling together all this information. It should also be its role to delegate to managers within the company who should contact which politicians. In football terms, who's marking whom?

So, for example, the company's president or chief operating officer may be delegated to contact either the prime minister, president or the secretary of state for the relevant department. The chief financial officer may be in touch with the treasury or the finance department of the government. The operations director may be in touch with the environment agency or other key government departments which have a responsibility for the operations of the company.

Communications at the regional level

This again needs to be decided in advance and can be delegated to the facility which is based in that particular region. For example, the general manager of a factory may be delegated to be in touch with the leader of the regional assembly. It is important that this manager, who may not have much public affairs experience, be fully briefed. Ideally, if he or she is a wise and far-seeing manager, he or she will have joined local organisations such as the chamber of commerce, which will allow him or her to 'rub shoulders' with these key people. In addition, he or she will put together a formal procedure, as outlined above, so that he or she has access at the highest levels when it is needed.

Communications at the community level

Again, this becomes the responsibility of the regional manager, with advice from the crisis management team and the public affairs department. A localised diagnostic (Chapter 11) would have been completed so that the key movers and shakers in the community are known and methodologies for contacting them are well understood and rehearsed. Again, good networking should ensure that there are personal contacts in place, so that in a crisis people can contact those who are affected and those who are affected have easy access to those who are managing the crisis.

The public

In the Oxfam and Nestlé case (Chapter 8), the NGO managed to generate 40,000 emails in a few days for Nestlé. This is the sort of level of intensity of communications one can expect in a real crisis.

As stated in Chapter 9, an organisation can expect to receive hundreds of phone calls in a very short period of time. To get information to the public, there are a number of mechanisms available which are now discussed.

The call centre

Organisations with large marketing or sales teams or a customer services department will, nowadays, almost certainly have a call centre. Generally these are linked into the email system so it is easy to get information to them quickly. Therefore the hymn sheet must be given to the call centre at the earliest point and they must be constantly updated. Naturally, they must also be trained in advance. They should then be able to handle calls in a quick and efficient manner.

The website

The website can be prepared in advance so that people can immediately access information. The crisis page must be linked – only during a crisis – to the home page for ease of access. The page for the public should be different from the page for the media, although the information is essentially the same. The media page will have more background information and, of course, for the more insistent members of the public, it is also available. It is important, however, that the media is seen to be treated more specially and differently from members of the general public.

Toll-free telephone numbers

Again, these need to be sourced and prepared well in advance and kept at the ready for when a crisis strikes. If it is possible to answer most queries, this information should be put on the toll-free number, before it is routed through to the call centre. Often a simple message will suffice.

Similarly, the organisation's main switchboard can have a message placed on it which gives simple basic information. For example: 'We are aware that we have had difficulties with power supplies in the central area. Our engineers are working on this and we hope to have electricity supplies returned to all people by midday at the latest.' This simple message satisfies the vast majority of people's need for information. They do not need to know the technical details about generators, power supplies or anything else. A point of detail: it is important to apply the maxim 'underpromise and overdeliver'. As it is likely that some people may still not have electricity until mid-afternoon, it is better to say that for all people.

Dealing with customers

At the height of a crisis, it is all too easy to forget one's customers and suppliers, what with the media, politicians and other exciting stakeholders to deal with. However, the media and political circus will move on and you are still left with a business to run.

Therefore, one part of the crisis team should be delegated to deal with customers and suppliers. Again, training and testing are important, as are key messages – from the hymn sheet. The customer relations department or similar is ideal to handle this.

The approach must be proactive. Contact them before they can worry about you. This illustrates a positive and proactive approach.

Restoring reputation after a crisis

Even if a company handles a crisis well, there will inevitably be some reputation damage. Most organisations tend to heave a sigh of relief when a crisis passes and do little else. However, just as after a storm, one replaces tiles on one's roof, then the storm damage of a crisis must also be repaired. Otherwise – and remember the second escalation – one risks losing the whole roof the next time a squall hits you.

Checklist for establishing your external communications in a crisis

In this chapter, along with Chapter 15, we have examined how to deal with the media, politicians, the public and your customers during a crisis. The checklist below can be used to determine which actions you need to take in regard to your external communications.

Factor	Yes/no	Action
1. Are all external communication channels – to the media, politicians, suppliers, the general public, customers and so on – effective, quick and operational?		
2. Do all these people know who to contact within your company and how to do so?		
3. Has a sample lifebelt statement been prepared?		
4. Has a sample Q&A sheet been prepared?		
5. Have internal spokespeople been identified and prepared?		
6. Has prior liaison with key media figures and so on been undertaken?		
7. Has a website or website link been prepared whereby members of the public can easily access information during a crisis?		
8. Have toll-free numbers been established that can be used by members of the public during a crisis?		

Conclusion

The public and its representatives must be handled well in a crisis, otherwise the mishandling itself can become a crisis. Remember your customers – after all they are your business, no matter what distractions take you away from them.

CHAPTER 18

Training, Testing and Refinement

Once the hard work has been completed, the plan is in place and the team is ready to go, it is almost time for a well-deserved break. However, these plans are still theoretical – they may not even work. Too many plans are based around what the company would like to happen in a crisis rather than what might happen. Remember Murphy.

These plans have only been simulated in the team's minds. To be effective and robust, they must be tested and tested hard. Then they must be refined and refined again. A plan which, once devised, is left like a bottle of fine wine will not mature, it will rot.

On paper the plans may appear to work fine. However, the real test would be in a crisis situation. During a real crisis is not the time to be testing procedures for the first time. There is little room for error. It is here that testing of procedures needs to play a key role.

Firstly, when setting out to test any crisis management procedures, it is important that any scenario which is used to test the plan is realistic. It is almost counterproductive if the scenario cannot be believed by its participants and makes learning difficult. These testing opportunities should not simply be taken as a matter of course, or approached as 'something which has to be done'. They are important learning initiatives, where improvements and problems can be drawn out to ensure both that the plan and its participants work well together and that, when a crisis hits, the majority of the bugs have already been ironed out.

Setting the scene

When running any crisis management scenario, an important objective is to have a clear understanding from the whole team about what they want to achieve from the exercise. What exactly do the team want to draw from the activity to make it worthwhile? This needs to be agreed. For example, the public affairs team may wish to test further their knowledge and skills of working with politicians on a national scale; internal communications may wish to look at how best to disseminate information in certain branches of the business. Whatever the objectives, it is important that these are agreed beforehand.

The next step is to pull away from the team slightly and begin to work up a scenario. Clearly, the team must not be aware of the scenario. When planning a scenario, almost like planning to write a play or television programme, the plotline, subplots and inputs need to be worked up carefully. After all, a crisis does not simply revolve around one small action, but the repercussions of a number of actions.

Crisis scenarios

For example, a scenario could be based on a recent fire in a large city that has damaged underground cables. This has led to the loss of both voice and data services to over 150,000 business and domestic users. The fire and damage to the tunnel is only part of the crisis. The real crisis revolves around those who have lost communications – ambulance, police, fire service, shops, offices and so on. It is these inputs that create the crisis atmosphere.

Generally a crisis scenario should last up to half a day and therefore the plot line needs to reflect this. It should be punchy and fast-paced, to mimic a real crisis. Generally, to put this together internally can take up to three months. Although time-consuming, it is essential.

Clearly there are a number of inputs which any crisis would have and these are based on the type of scenario. However, the following inputs can be taken and adapted to any number of scenarios to test communication and management procedures.

Telephone roles

The first action by the majority of people in a crisis is to pick up the phone. Without an effective filtering process, what goes through and what doesn't? How are calls rated and who deals with them? These inputs can be simulated by members of staff who are not part of the crisis management team. However, as the scenario needs to be kept secret, it is often better to hire, say, students, to simulate the roles. A number of roles and situations can be devised to ensure that the crisis team are kept on their toes. Some example roles are:

- Employee
- Union representative
- Neighbour
- Local politician
- Local newspaper reporter
- Customer
- Supplier
- Building agent
- Community association representative
- Local businesses.

For our fire example, some roles might be:

- *David Simmons, red button support:* Without the telephone lines, old people living in sheltered accommodation can no longer call for support if they get into trouble.
- *Judith Baker, local baker:* Will the company pay her mobile telephone bill while she has to use it for business?
- *James Hack,* Evening News *reporter:* How long did the fire go undetected? How long until communications are restored?
- *Joan Keley, employee on the scene:* Is the smoke toxic? Are there any live wires in the tunnel? The fire brigade want to know.
- *Jack Rush – local ambulance man:* Will he able to use his radio-based system if he brings a patient to the hospital?

Each character has a different agenda and should be briefed before the course. Each operator can have a number of different roles throughout the scenario – usually about 40 roles can be embellished by the operators.

The role of these operators is to ensure that each member of the crisis team and their support teams is regularly engaged by an external force (in a real-life crisis, they would also have internal calls to deal with, so they have an advantage in that all the decision makers are in one room). This means that there is the need for a number of role-players to keep the team members on their toes. These will be providing constant interruptions. They should have the names of each of the delegates and will be able to ring and demand to speak to team participants by name.

The media

With all crises, it does not take long for the media to become involved and this should be reflected in the scenario. The influence of the media is usually split into two inputs – the journalist and news pieces.

Journalist and media team

A media team, comprised of a professional journalist and a cameraman with a small camcorder, should be used to circulate around the participants to doorstep members of the team. With the plethora of 24-hour news channels broadcasting 'live from the scene', the camera crew turning up on the doorstep is no longer expensive and their arrival at the scene of a crisis is much more likely than it was ten years ago. It certainly makes the news more interesting and accessible. Hence dealing with a journalist face to face, rather than simply by telephone, is becoming a matter of course.

The journalist should initiate contact and demand live interviews. He or she will be around at all times, reacting to leaks and news as it develops. Statements – either in writing or oral – will be demanded from the team and the media centre or press office.

News pieces

With the media, the two most visible presences likely while a crisis unfolds are print and television. Ideally, pre-recorded television bulletins are a practical and useful input, reflecting today's TV news society. Producing these – including finding willing volunteers and producing scripts – can be time-consuming, but they are worthwhile and bring a live edge.

These can be accompanied or replaced by print media articles; however, the responsiveness of the print media is drastically reduced, because there is generally only one edition of a newspaper a day. This hinders the ability to react or be updated as the crisis escalates. The news pieces play important parts, used to escalate the crisis to the next level. The following extract is from the telecom tunnel fire story:

> A major cable fire has brought chaos to the region as emergency services struggle to cope with a communication blackout. According to the local news,

emergency services have been stranded after the fire damaged vital communication links to the heart of the city.

The city ambulance and fire service said it was struggling after the fire damaged its radio network. Other emergency services have also been hit. Because of the scale of this fire and the number of connections that have been wiped out, there are concerns that residents will be unable to access vital emergency services.

At this early stage it's impossible to gauge the full extent of the incident, which has seen the loss of more than 130,000 telephone lines. From banks to airlines, it seems the fire has brought many companies to their knees, with many businesses relying on mobile phones and courier services to keep business flowing.

It is important to keep escalating the story during the crisis scenario, reflecting what would happen in real life. For example, our scenario might progress thus to the next plateau:

A major mobile phone operator in the area of the recent city fire has said that some of its network had been hit and that it's working to reroute calls elsewhere because of the loss of connection to the national network and the sheer volume of calls creating network congestion.

Hosting services have also been hit, as a statement on a national bank website reads: 'We're sorry but the website is currently unavailable. This is due to a major telecommunications failure in the west of the country. We're working hard to restore the service as soon as possible.' The loss of the website brings the loss of access to accounts held online – an inconvenience to customers who rely on Internet banking to manage their accounts.

Fire crews are still dealing with the incident deep down in tunnels beneath the centre of the city. Black smoke is reportedly billowing out as firefighters use emergency generators to ventilate the tunnels and try to tackle the blaze.

The news pieces should also include interviews conducted with the various characters of the scenario (activists, employees, local politicians) to constantly feed new angles and issues into the scenario requiring immediate action. They will update the situation and give new information. Everything that could, or could not, go wrong will go wrong, but it is important that the scenario remains believable. Remember, no one would have predicted or thought that a scenario based on the tragic September 11 events would have been believable, but it happened and the consequences were very real.

The loose cannon

Anyone now with an Internet connection, or simply a PC, can have a fully fledged action group up and running within minutes. People power is still surprisingly strong across the world, as disillusionment with the political system begins to set in and voter apathy increases.

In a David versus Goliath battle, everyone enjoys backing the David character. In any scenario, activists, opponent or otherwise, will find their way into the crisis to become a nuisance and an instant media pundit. They are ready to be interviewed on camera and fill in any vacuum of information which the company might leave. They should be loud, proud and very outspoken in order to keep the group on their toes. Their response to our unfolding scenario might be:

> This situation simply highlights the shocking underinvestment by this once great public utility in the hands of a privatised and money-grabbing market.

The expert

During any crisis, there will be a request for external information. Rather than taking up valuable internal resources (and possibly confusing various employees with a 'scenario'), some of this should be produced already and an expert should be part of the scenario team and should be the key contact for further information or passing messages along.

This 'expert', as with most people in a crisis, can be difficult to pin down on exact meanings, implications and even for a conversation. Correspondence would be full of technical jargon and 'ifs', 'buts' and 'maybes'. Information from the expert should be produced beforehand by a real internal 'expert' for authenticity. This is an example of what could be said:

> A fire in deep level tunnels running beneath the streets of the city caused extensive damage to cables and widespread disruption to phone and broadband services in the surrounding area.

> The fire is affecting some 150,000 homes and businesses in the centre of the city. We are currently assessing the extent of the damage and working to reroute and restore as many of these services as possible.

However, the true extent of the repair will not become clear until the fire authority have declared the tunnel safe and allow engineers access. It is not possible at this stage to say how long it will be until services are restored to normal. A great deal of testing will still have to be carried out on the network.

The timetable

Compiling these elements into a believable plot can be difficult, but quite fun. Eventually you may have a timetable which reflects the following:

09.00   Crisis scenario starts (unknown to participants) with a telephone call from the crisis coordinator and they have been asked to assemble. No more information is available at present

Start of telephone calls, faxes and emails which will continue throughout the exercise

09:15   Journalist and cameraman arrive downstairs – the media want an interview immediately about the situation

09:25   Group director arrives and attempts to become involved, comes in and out of the room throughout the exercise

09:30   News bulletin on the TV

09:45   Head of international operations arrives, comes in and out of the room throughout the exercise

09:50   Activist turns up and demands immediate explanations. Further calls for press interviews from journalists

10:00   First technical update brief

10:15   Manufacturing department calls re going into crisis mode

10:30   News bulletin on the TV – interview with engineering department spokesman (very evasive)

Regulatory body calls re local government notification

TV crew arrive for interview

10:45   Media telephone to request to run a forum (with the mayor, activist and crisis team) on the crisis

10:45   Call from company expert – there is a delay in the technical brief

11:00   Activist turns up again in the foyer claiming there is a cover-up

11:00   10-page update is received

Further escalation
News bulletin on the TV

Regulatory body becomes involved; hints at retribution for the company

TV crew conduct interview with activist in lobby

11:15   Press department issues general statement that some of the allegations may be correct

Newspaper article is received, further escalation

11:40   TV crew/journalist arrives for press conference

12:00   Press conference

Clearly, to gain best value from these exercises, it may also be worthwhile considering working with the business continuity team, to ensure that communications between the teams, and the company as a whole, are working towards a consistent message.

Checklist – materials

Rules of engagement

An outline of the scenario and rules specific to the testing procedure – persons within the company they can and cannot call to ensure the test does not escalate. This should be left in the crisis room.

Roles

Roles should be produced for telephone roles, journalist, activist and expert to ensure they are updated with the scenario and can move the story forward at certain points. It is important to train those who are playing roles some time beforehand so they can become familiar with their characters.

Update briefs

These briefs are written reports updating the team on the current situation and any further news which has developed. These should be distributed periodically.

Background material

Any additional background material which may be required to fill the story and allow it to become believable and ensure that the team has the facts to hand that they would have in a crisis.

Debrief

Any testing exercise is only as good as the debriefing session afterwards and the learning drawn from this. It is essential that even the smallest problems are picked up on, from note taking to communications, which is often one of the areas where most crisis management procedures fall down.

This debriefing session should review procedures and outputs, looking at what could be improved in the future. The general topics of discussion should be:

- *Procedures* – how did they work? Could they be improved?
- *Communication* – was this effective? How good was the record keeping and messaging aspect of the team's work?
- *Record keeping* – did this work effectively and were actions recorded and followed up swiftly?
- *Resources* – does the team have the right resources and is it making effective use of what it has to hand?
- *Team members* – does the team require any more members, or members of a different expertise on hand to offer assistance?
- *Contact externally and internally* – were the messages consistent? Are there any suggested ways of improving how conversations are held or messages relayed – particularly in respect of the media?

These points are important and allow the team to build on the expertise they have and the training. From this, the handbook and procedures should be updated almost immediately. The longer this takes, the more value is lost from the exercise – learning must be captured and implemented quickly. Refinements should be discussed and distributed for comment within the next few days, so that the team has time to think about possible solutions – rather than implementing them in an adrenaline rush.

It is important that these are held at least once a year, or when a new member has to join the team. After all, it pays to be prepared.

Checklist for training, testing and refinement

The checklist below will help you to prepare for testing your procedures.

Factor	Yes/No	Action
1. Have the crisis management procedures at your company been tested?		
2. Are all CMT members clear and in agreement as to the aims and objectives of the testing?		
3. Has a crisis scenario been designed and carried out to test procedures?		
4. Have areas of improvement been identified?		
5. Has the learning been captured and procedures updated and implemented?		
6. Have all team members, including support teams, been trained as to the new procedures?		
7. Has another dry run been organised?		

CHAPTER 19

Business Continuity

When a crisis hits, you need to be able to carry on with your business. A crisis can have serious consequences on your revenue streams. Shell sales in Germany fell 30 per cent in a month during *Brent Spar*; Perrier sales halved. A crisis can be most damaging to the revenue stream – the most fragile part of any business. Tackling the crisis, managing third party advocates and trying to ensure that there is one consistent message is an important part of brand reputation. But what is a brand if there is no way to sell the product or service?

It is this business continuity process that needs to be given just as much attention as managing the crisis itself. If the crisis is more than a branding issue and affects the day-to-day working of a company, it will begin to drain the company. Companies not producing goods still have to pay bills, pay staff and have obligations to consumers and customers. It is these processes that an effective business continuity plan aims to encapsulate and address.

A matter of survival

When it comes to a crisis – from a natural disaster to trading difficulties – all businesses need to know what they would do if such an event were to strike. More importantly, however, all businesses should know how they would survive the next few hours, days, weeks or months it would take to restore normal systems and ways of working and so meet its obligations as a business.

It is a sad fact, however, that most businesses believe that this will never happen to them, and possibly quite rightly so. Such events are rare, and often small enough to be addressed while business continues as usual.

What could possibly happen to threaten the future of a successful business? Here is one chilling fact. More than 40 per cent of companies affected by a terrorist bombing in the heart of Manchester went out of business – for good. An unfortunate, unpreventable and unpredictable event. However, its ramifications spread much further – damaging businesses in a way and style no one in the area had seen before or was prepared for. For the majority of people watching events unfold through the media, it had an emotional effect, but very little material effect. However, for those businesses with damaged properties, goods and services, livelihoods were suddenly in jeopardy. Those with larger cash reserves were able to survive, while smaller businesses found themselves in an impossible situation from which many were unable to recover.

As terrorism climbs high on the political and economic agenda, it is easy to focus on such events, especially as statistics show that 90 per cent of the disaster relief relating to 9/11 went to small businesses and 10 per cent went to homeowners. Although a commercial area was badly hit, it was the businesses which needed the most help. This event unravelled the unfortunate truth – those who do not plan ahead for such contingencies will fail. It boils down to survival of the fattest – those with the biggest cash reserves.

With this gloomy scenario, it is easy to think that a large sum of money in the bank may save any company. Indeed it will certainly help to cushion the blow, but is this its wisest use? Is it all about the money, or simply clever planning? As businesses become more dependent on elements such as technology, it becomes more critical to have a disaster recovery plan.

A 2004 survey showed that the top reason for European countries taking an interest in business continuity was the realisation that they relied heavily on IT to remain in business. The common misconception was that in this world of anti-terrorism initiatives, it is the fear of terror that rules the agenda. However, only France (12 per cent), the UK (10 per cent) and Italy (6 per cent) cited September 11 or the threat of terrorism as a factor that made the board put business continuity on the priority list.

Planning ahead

If a terrifying event, such as a major crisis, was unfortunately to befall a company – what could be done? How could the problem be overcome? With no planning or forethought, it is quite simply back to the beginning and by the time the business is closed or partially functioning, it is haemorrhaging money.

It does not have to be an enormous task, after all most businesses take such measures automatically, almost as common sense – the most obvious being to back-up the data from the company's computer servers. However, this is all well and good if it was the data that were affected by any crisis, but what if it were the machines, the building, the personnel, facilities and so on? What would happen then?

It doesn't really matter what the crisis might be, what matters is that steps are taken to prepare the company. The first step is to look towards putting together a business continuity plan. Like a crisis management plan, this needs to be prepared in advance and procedures reviewed regularly. The plans can be put together simultaneously and, in the event of a disaster or crisis, the procedures can quickly be put in place to ensure that the business is able to stand up and fight.

Business continuity planning typically involves an assessment of business needs and impacts, recovery strategies and a framework plan. This planning process enables companies to take a close look at the business and put together thoughts which are designed to be robust enough to cover the loss of business-critical procedures and infrastructure. Put quite simply, the business continuity plan is a way to work around problems which may occur and simply be out of the control of the company and employees.

Most organisations are reliant on just a few key departments for the lifeblood of the corporation – a head office and administrative building, production facilities and information technology systems. Stripped down, this is the bare bones of most businesses today. Every business relies on these factors to keep it alive.

People, quite obviously, are key to any company, but are often overlooked as a resource. Systems and physical assets are the management tools which help the business perform and provide for its customers. This is a finely balanced triangle. A breakdown in just one of these sides can lead to degradation of the management structure and the business. Even a crisis as simple as a fire in a workplace could have huge ramifications on the structure of the company.

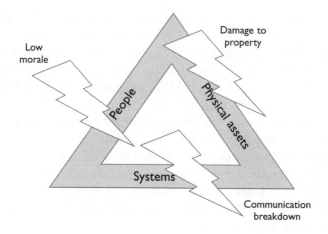

An example of such a reliance on assets is IT. It is hard to believe businesses survived without computers but, at one time, they did. A 2003 survey showed that one in five companies has seen a downtime in IT services of at least one working day. For a typical company, an outage longer than this is simply not an option. It is relied on for communication, systems and is a key physical asset.

However, business have streamlined and adapted, with computers removing the pools of resources that companies would employ for the simplest of tasks – services replaced with software. But could any company work efficiently and effectively without them today? With IT being as unpredictable as ever, how long could any business last without either its data or software?

In a survey which asked what disaster companies across Europe most feared, all respondents, except those in the UK, said 'hardware failure'. UK businesses appear to have a deep-seated fear of fire, with 36 per cent of respondents saying that the company going up in flames was the thing that concerned them most. In reality, only 4 per cent of businesses experienced downtime due to fire and, with fire and safety systems constantly improving, this will no doubt continue to decrease. However, when it comes to company downtime, the biggest culprit is software failure, with 21 per cent of UK businesses suffering from IT-related problems.

In France and Sweden, most were concerned with hardware failure. However, it was power failure that had been the biggest cause of system downtime. It is not the actual risk that makes us prepared – it is what we perceive as the risks that motivates us. Therefore, any business continuity plan needs to be able to cope with a number of different crises and eventualities, not just a handful of specific scenarios. As Murphy's Law states: It will be a completely different disaster which will affect the company.

Business continuity should not simply be viewed as something a business will look at once it reaches a certain size. Granted, the larger the organisation, the more vulnerable it may become but, conversely, the more resources it can draw on. Like it or not, there are a number of key parts of any organisation – large or small – which, if they went down, would bring the company down with them. In terms of continuity planning, just as in planning for a crisis, it pays to be prepared. A total of 37% of chief financial officers (CFOs) said they perceive their firms to be most vulnerable in the area of disaster recovery. This was followed by security of information systems, cited by 24 per cent of CFOs. This, for a number of reasons, is a very startling and worrying figure.

Business continuity planning is not a complicated science, nor does it require a large team of consultants to produce and prepare. The purpose of any business continuity plan is to ensure that the business recovers effectively and relatively unscathed from a disaster or crisis and is able to continue to operate. The plan, similar to a crisis management plan, needs to include the actions that should to be taken to restore operations to their pre-disaster level, by whom and in what timeframe.

THE MILLENNIUM BUG – Y2K

The Y2K bug was potentially a ticking time bomb for all major computer applications. The computer and system application companies came out with year 2000 compliant operating systems and system software. IT companies around the world spent billions of dollars to go through their entire application source code to look for the Y2K bug and fix it. Almost everybody raced to make themselves Y2K compliant before the fast approaching deadline.

Finally when the big day came, many utilities and other companies switched off their main computers and put the backup computers to work. When the clock ticked January 1 2000, no major problems were reported. Almost every bank worked fine, no major power outages were reported, aeroplanes still flew and the whole world went on with its normal life.

Analysis
Would this have happened without the vast amount of money and time put behind it? Perhaps, perhaps not, but the risk was assessed, plans were put in place to ensure business continuity and it worked.

Creating business continuity plans

The first step in putting together a business continuity plan is to ensure firstly that the process has buy-in and the benefits of such an approach are known to management. This process can be time-consuming to set up, but once the groundwork is completed, like the crisis management plan, it is easy to maintain.

Assembling a business continuity management team, parallel to the crisis management team and probably with some common members, is essential. Each of the main business and operational areas within the organisation should be represented in the project team, in a similar fashion to the crisis management team. In most cases, the membership should not be identical; however, in smaller companies this may be unavoidable.

Each representative from these key business areas should have a comprehensive understanding of how their department functions, key risk areas and also a broader view of how this fits into the company as a whole. As with the crisis management team, this does not necessarily have to be the most senior person available. In fact, it is often better that the positions are not taken by these people, as initially the time needed to set up such a programme may not lend itself to those in such positions. The business continuity team should see itself as a broad mix, with numbers restricted to a maximum of eight key people. This team, however, can call on additional members from across the company, should they be required in setting up the plan and piecing together the information.

The first meeting of the team needs preparation to be effective. Each representative needs to be aware of a number of factors in each of their operational areas:

- *Mission-critical areas and procedures:* Which parts of respective departments, if removed, would stop the businesses from functioning effectively? Thinking laterally is key – IT is an obvious choice, but what about personnel suffering from access problems, a flooded building, technical outage regarding phone lines, a wildcat strike affecting the postal system? All these can, and will, occur at one stage or another.
- *Operational and administrative procedures:* How does each department work with other departments? Every company is a unique web, with inputs and outputs flowing to and from departments. If one of these departments were to be disrupted, what would be the effect on the surrounding organisation?
- *Existing procedures:* The problem with producing new procedures is that they can often contradict other areas and procedures. In today's companies, there exists a myriad of red tape which also has to be taken into account. However, do not let this area become too restrictive, after all, these circumstances are exceptional. Regulations regarding health and safety and evacuation procedures will clearly need to be followed.

Once this information has been assembled, the business continuity plan can begin to take shape. Although starting such a document can seem a daunting task, it is essential. If a first draft is not completed at the beginning, it will certainly have to be done so under much more pressured circumstances at a later date.

Other useful, but not essential, documents for a business continuity team are:

- Organisational chart showing names and positions of employees
- Staff emergency contact details
- List of suppliers and contact numbers
- List of professional advisers and emergency contact information
- List of emergency services and contact numbers
- Premises layouts, maps and addresses
- IT specifications and inventories
- Insurance information
- Asset inventories.

The first meeting will be an onerous and at times worrying task. Like running over the details of funeral arrangements, simulating the demise of the company may seem morbid, but being prepared for the worst-case scenario is key.

The key to the business continuity plan is that it should be, as with the crisis management plan, easy to use, easily accessible and containing only useful information and procedures. At each inclusion, the question must be asked: Is this essential to the running of the business? Do I need to say this? Will we require this information? Is it in its simplest form possible? If the answer is no, do not include it. The last thing you need in any situation is to have to sift through irrelevant regulations to get to what you want.

The team needs to consider its business-critical systems, communication mechanisms and performance during a number of possible disruptions. By running your business through a number of scenarios, you can build up a picture of how these processes can be managed and disruption overcome.

Physical and IT security measures are also important. Is the building open to the public? What measures are in place to ensure that it is secured at night or when the building is not in use? The same goes for computer security: do staff have passwords taped to monitors? Are portable computers secured at the end of the day? Is a suitable virus scanner and backup facility in place? During the exercise, there will be a number of such elements which might be able to be addressed straightaway – which is one obvious business benefit there and then.

Running our design and print company, Design Unlimited, through the scenario, would create a table similar to that below.

Storm	Risk Area	Business Effects	Rating
	Flooding or damage to hardware	Inability to design using CAD	5
	Staff access difficulties	Possible closure of branch	5
	Disruption of power	Inability to design, work, process payments or invoices. No backup power available.	5
	Minor damage to building, for example broken window	Some minor disruptions during repair and clean-up	2
	Disruption of telephones	Inability to make and receive calls, faxes, Internet access	3
	Major damage to building	Loss of access to building	5
	Disruption to suppliers	Reliance on suppliers is medium – alternative suppliers are easily sourced	1

The rating is based on the effect on business revenue. It is important not to lose sight of the aim of this exercise and the resulting plan is to ensure that the revenue stream to the company is not disrupted.

Other scenarios with equally complex effects are snow, fire, subsidence, contamination, loss of power through to the more obscure effects of a health scare and civil unrest. Obscure they may be, but they can be crippling to any business.

From this list, the vulnerabilities of the organisation are considered in a variety of situations. By role-playing – albeit only on paper for the moment – and talking through the effects of such crises, a number of commonalities regarding loss of functions in a business will be uncovered.

The output from this meeting should be a table, as above, listing a variety of scenarios and their effects on the business. From here, the next step is to consider what can be done about them.

It is not how it happens, but what happens

Once this exercise is completed, the basis of the business continuity plan is established.

The format of the plan needs to be agreed for each section in order to give the handbook consistency. Each team should then produce its own section, looking at risk areas, contacts and resources required in the event of an emergency. Look outwards as well as inwards for the resources, but it is important to ensure that there is not too much overlap between departments.

Each plan needs a manager who will direct the plan and its utilisation. This role, ideally, should be duplicated within the team to ensure that absence does not bring the plan down at the first hurdle.

Each section should look at:

■ *Team role:* What the team usually does in relation to operations within the company. An overview of its inputs, outputs, management structure and personnel.

■ *Location information:* Information about the current location of the department, equipment, access, floor plans and so on.

■ *Backup plans:* Existing backup procedures, names and contacts for those who carry them out. Information regarding evacuation plans and existing disaster plans.

■ *Contacts:* Contact information for:
  ■ Plan coordinator
  ■ Emergency services
  ■ Suppliers
  ■ Contractors
  ■ Key customers
  ■ Insurance details
  ■ Management personnel
  ■ Staff emergency contact numbers
  ■ Building maintenance.

■ *Key areas and priorities:* A list of actions which should be taken if the department has a failure – backing up of data, contact of key clients and so on.

■ *Business continuity:* Plans for the loss of business-critical functions, including agreed outside contractors, alternative locations, trained members of staff able to take over specific roles and so on. The contact number of the crisis management team coordinator should also be in this section, as with the numbers of the whole team.

■ *Activity log:* Basic log to record actions of team.

This forms the basis of any business continuity plan. It is important that general employees know of its existence, rather than its details. It is a document which will evolve over time and be built upon thorough testing –

in real circumstances and through general training, as identified with the crisis management plan. It should be updated at least once a year and preferably on a quarterly basis, as businesses and events can change beyond recognition in just six months. However, once the document has been produced, this is not a difficult task.

The plan should be integrated with the crisis management handbook outlined earlier – a lot of the key themes and responsibilities will be mirrored and reflected in each team and document and therefore it may be worthwhile completing the projects in parallel.

Checklist for ensuring business continuity

It is imperative to ensure that your business continuity procedures work together with your crisis management procedures. The questions asked in the checklist below will help you in instigating your business continuity procedures.

Factor	Yes/no	Action
1. Has your company designed and implemented business continuity procedures?		
2. Has a business continuity team been assembled?		
3. Has an easy to use and easily accessible business continuity plan been formed which contains only useful and relevant information and procedures?		
4. Does this plan work alongside the crisis management procedures?		
5. Do the CMT and the business continuity team work alongside one another?		

Conclusion

Business continuity is a parallel and then a sequential stage of crisis management planning. Whereas crisis management is a form of fire-fighting, business continuity is rebuilding and ensuring survival. Both are vital for business success.

INDEX

Page numbers in italics indicate case studies

A

accidents 3, 8–9
  to aircraft *3–4, 41, 74–5*
activists 64–71
  see also non-governmental
    organisations (NGOs)
aggressive attitude in a crisis 37
aircraft accidents *3–4, 41, 74–5*
Air France *74–5*
alliances, need for 35, 93
Allied Irish Bank (AIB) *49*
al-Qaeda *54, 55–6*
altruism 50
aluminium *21*
Alzheimer's disease *21*
anthrax *31–2*
arrogance, in crisis management 36
asylum seekers *52–3*

B

banks, *see* Allied Irish Bank; Halifax
  Bank
Braer 24
Brent Spar 10–17, 19–20, 25
  crisis curve 10–17
  and Greenpeace *12–17*, 27, 46, 48
  third party advocates (TPAs) 91, *92–3*
British Airways, strikes *145–6*
British Midland *41*
'business as usual' attitude in a crisis 37
business continuity 165–74
  checklist 174
  creating plans 169–74

crisis management handbook and
  172–3, 174
forward planning 166–9
revenue stream 165, 172
risk perception 168–9
security 171
survival 165–6
butterfly 98, 111, 112, 113, 117

C

California, power cuts *59–60*
call centres 114–15, 152
Chernobyl *8–9*
chief executive (CEO)
  ideal role 40
  letters to employees 145, 149
  as primary PR source 131–2
  role in a crisis 38–41, 96–7
Coca-Cola *51*
communication(s)
  community level 151
  dealing with non-governmental
    organisations (NGOs) 70–1
  effective use of 81
  external, checklist 153–4
  failure of 58
  government level 151
  internal, *see* communications, internal
  mixed messages 100–1
  with public 152–3
  regional level 151
  routes of 58–9
  testing 150
communications, internal 141–9
  CEO's letters to employees 145, 149
  checklist 149
  crisis management teams and 100

Index